EDINBURGH & THE BORDERS

Landscape Heritage

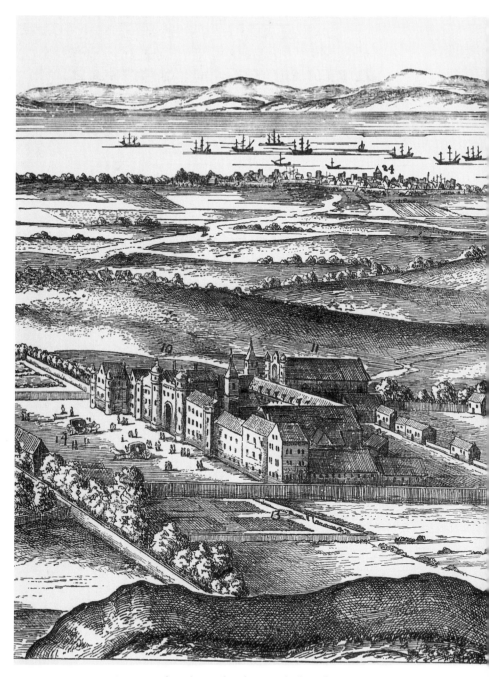

A view of Holyrood Palace, Edinburgh, in 1670.
The palace was set in virtually open countryside

EDINBURGH & THE BORDERS
Landscape Heritage

Ian Whyte

Series Editor:
Allan Patmore

DAVID & CHARLES
Newton Abbot   London

For Richard Gillanders
who explored so much of this area with me

Landscape Heritage

Other titles in this series:

THE LAKE DISTRICT
Edited by William Rollinson

THE NORTH YORK MOORS
Edited by D. A. Spratt and B. J. D. Harrison

Photographs by the author unless credited otherwise

British Library Cataloguing in Publication Data
Whyte, I. D. (Ian D.)
 Edinburgh and the Borders: landscape heritage.
 1. Edinburgh, history   2. Scotland. Border country.
 Local history
 I. Title
 941.34

 ISBN 0–7153–9236–0

Typeset by Typesetters (Birmingham) Ltd
Smethwick, West Midlands
and printed in Great Britain
by Redwood Press Ltd, Melksham
for David & Charles plc
Brunel House   Newton Abbot   Devon

CONTENTS

CONTENTS

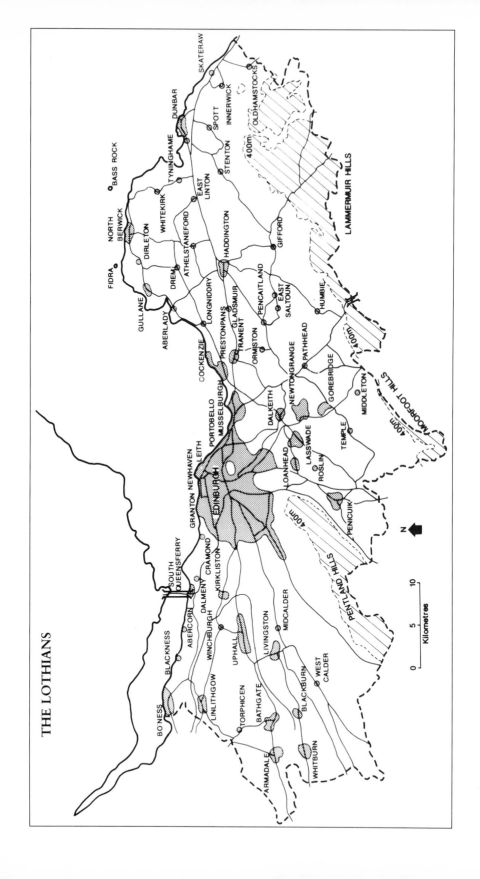

THE LOTHIANS

Kilometres
0   5   10

N

INTRODUCTION

THIS is the first volume in the Landscape Heritage series to venture north of the Border. It differs from its predecessors in some important respects. The area which this book covers is much larger than English regions like the Lake District or the North York Moors. It encompasses the modern local government regions of the Lothians and the Borders, or the older counties of East, Mid and West Lothian, Berwickshire, Roxburgh, Selkirk and Peebles. The city of Edinburgh, whose townscape is rich and complex, is dealt with in two separate chapters. The area is also extremely diverse ranging from the coastal plains of the Lothians and the drumlin country of the Berwickshire Merse to the hills of upper Tweeddale with their glacially deepened valleys and crags. In between lies a range of valleys, moors and uplands with varied physical features and human landscapes.

Another difference relates to the status of landscape history north of the Border. The English volumes in the Landscape Heritage series are innovative in many ways. Nevertheless, they build on an established tradition of research into the landscape. In Scotland far less is known about the development of the landscape and much less research has been undertaken. Moreover, although historians, archaeologists, place name specialists and others have made major contributions to our understanding of particular aspects of human activity in Scotland there have been few overviews of the evolution of the landscape itself.

The reasons for this are varied. One problem is the lack of Scottish documentary sources before the sixteenth and seventeenth centuries. Compared with England the medieval record is sparse. The scope for matching evidence in the early medieval charters with the modern landscape, which has been a feature of English landscape history in recent years, is extremely limited for Scotland. However, the documentary record is not as impoverished as has sometimes been suggested and many sources which may shed light on the landscape have yet to be exploited. This neglect has also been due to a persistent belief that the Scottish countryside was so thoroughly transformed

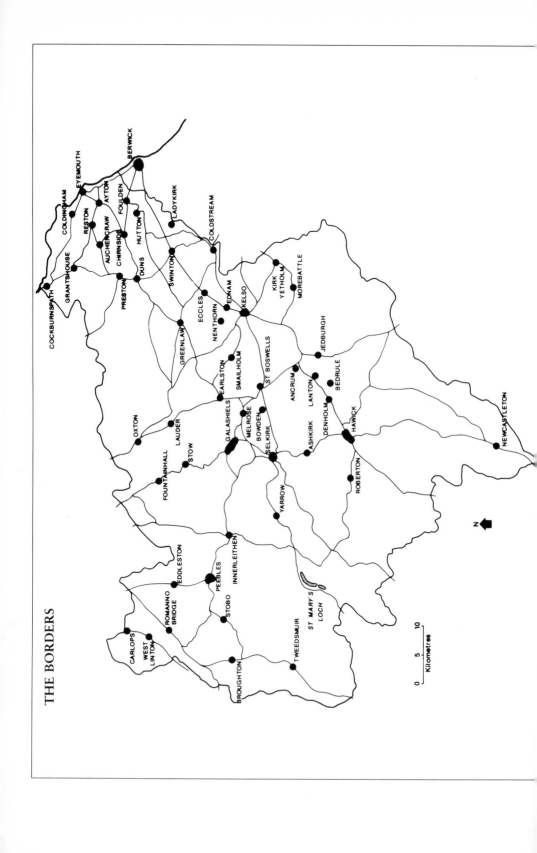

THE BORDERS

COCKBURNSPATH
COLDINGHAM
EYEMOUTH
AYTON
FOULDEN
LADYKIRK
RESTON
AUCHENCRAW
HUTTON
GRANTSHOUSE
CHIRNSIDE
COLDSTREAM
PRESTON
DUNS
SWINTON
GREENLAW
ECCLES
NENTHORN
EDNAM
KELSO
KIRK YETHOLM
MOREBATTLE
OXTON
EARLSTON
SMAILHOLM
ST BOSWELLS
JEDBURGH
LAUDER
GALASHIELS
MELROSE
BOWDEN
ANCRUM
LANTON
BEDRULE
STOW
SELKIRK
ASHKIRK
DENHOLM
HAWICK
NEWCASTLETON
FOUNTAINHALL
YARROW
ROBERTON
EDDLESTON
PEEBLES
INNERLEITHEN
ST MARY'S LOCH
ROMANNO BRIDGE
STOBO
CARLOPS
WEST LINTON
BROUGHTON
TWEEDSMUIR

N

0   5   10
Kilometres

by the Improvers in the later eighteenth and nineteenth centuries that relatively little of the pre-existing landscape has survived. As this volume will show, the pace and scale of landscape change under the impact of the Improvers was certainly great. Nevertheless, more of the pre-Improvement landscape remains than has often been suspected. The scope for further fieldwork is immense!

From a map point of view most of the area lies within the 100km National Grid square NT. To avoid repetition, all six-figure grid references to sites within this square have had the letters omitted. The description of any site does not guarantee right of access to it. Although landowners and farmers are generally amenable in allowing people to walk over unimproved land, outside the grouse shooting season, it is as well to seek permission before venturing off a public road. Visitors should adhere to the country code and take care to avoid inconveniencing the local inhabitants.

Finally, I would like to express my gratitude to Owen Tucker for drawing the maps and to members of the Media Services unit at Lancaster University for help with the photographs.

Ian Whyte,
1989

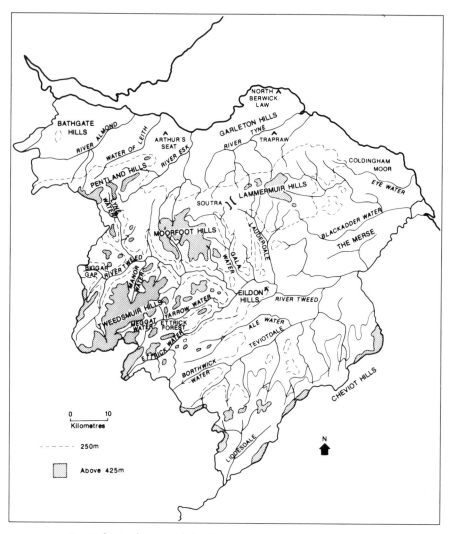

Fig 1 The Lothians and the Borders: topography and drainage

1
LANDSCAPE
WITHOUT FIGURES

THIS book is mainly concerned with how the landscape of south-east Scotland has developed under the influence of man. However, it is important to appreciate what the landscape was like before man appeared and how it has affected human activities since then. To understand how the scenery of the Lothians and the Borders has been formed a good starting point is to look at how geology has shaped the topography of the area. This includes both the solid rocks which form the skeleton of the country and the mantle of superficial deposits which covers them like a skin.

ROCKS AND SCENERY

To appreciate the main elements of the geology of this area it is worth taking in the view, on a clear day, from any of the small rocky crags of the Lothians: Edinburgh Castle Rock is probably the easiest to scale! To east and west the Lothian plain extends, interrupted by isolated volcanic hills. To the south are the Pentland Hills, but beyond them (to the east) a long blue line, the escarpment of the Moorfoots and the Lammermuirs, marks the start of the Border Hills. This is the true dividing line between the Lowlands and the Borders, between arable and pastoral-oriented farming, and often (in the past) between a settled society and a more warlike unruly one. It is also a significant geological divide between two of the main structural provinces of Scotland. To the north are the Central Lowlands, a rift valley produced by movements between two great fracture zones in the earth's crust. The steep northward face of the Border hills marks the line of one of these zones, where earth movements have brought older, more resistant Ordovician and Silurian rocks up against younger, more easily eroded sediments from the Old Red Sandstone and Carboniferous eras. The Southern Uplands have, in the past, been raised into a great mountain chain,

13

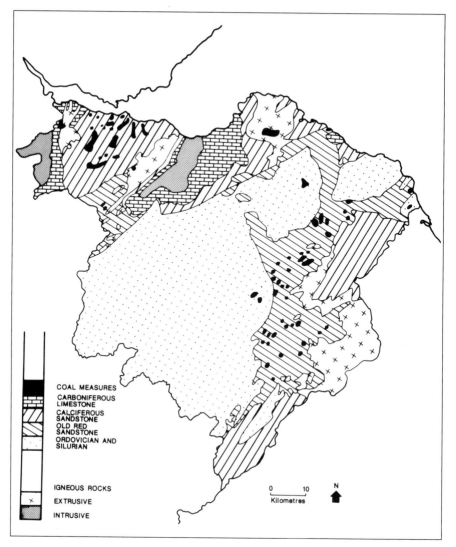

Fig 2 The Lothians and the Borders: geology

worn down, then uplifted once more to take their present form.

The Southern Uplands are composed mainly of Silurian and Ordovician greywacke, a sandstone hardened by the effects of heat. Because the thinly-bedded strata have been intensely folded, no single band of rock is exposed over a sufficiently large area to affect the form of the land surface. The result is a landscape of sweeping curves and rounded hills which are rarely rugged or precipitous. Different parts of the Border hills vary in character though. They reach their highest points around the head of the Tweed where more than a dozen summits rise to over 760m (2,500ft). They are separated by deeply-cut valleys like Talla, Gameshope and Fruid, which have been

14

deepened and steepened by the erosive effects of glaciers. St Mary's Loch, to the east of these hills, occupies a rock basin that has been gouged out by ice. Further east the hills decrease in height and boldness. The Moorfoots form a level plateau into which valleys are deeply cut. The Lammermuirs are a lower plateau with less sharply incised valleys. The Cheviots are different in their geology, being made up of volcanic lavas and granite, although their topography differs very little from the Tweeddale hills.

The Pentland Hills, whose northern slopes dominate Edinburgh, are an eroded anticline or arch of rocks from which the overlying softer Carboniferous strata have been removed, exposing a core of lavas and sediments of Old Red Sandstone age. As their summits are separated by low passes they have never been a major barrier to movement. The eastern margins of the Pentlands are particularly sharp because a major fault line brings their harder rocks up against the softer sediments of the Midlothian coal basin. The Pentlands really belong to the Central Lowlands although topographically they may seem a northward extension of the Border hills.

The lowlands of the Lothians and the Merse are punctuated by a series of volcanic hills. Edinburgh has spread around a group of them. As well as the Castle Rock there is Calton Hill dominating the eastern end of Princes Street and the rocky summits of Arthur's Seat and Salisbury Crags. Further away are Corstorphine Hill, the Craiglockhart Hills, Blackford Hill and the Braid Hills. Some of these crags are volcanic necks, plugs of hardened basalt or agglomerate left in the vents of long-vanished volcanoes. The Castle Rock, North Berwick Law, The Bass Rock and Arthur's Seat are good examples. Others, like Salisbury Crags, and Corstorphine Hill are sills or sheets of lava which have been intruded between the bedding planes of sedimentary rocks. Summits like Traprain Law and Black Hill in the Pentlands are laccoliths, domes of lava intruded among sedimentary rocks at great depth and are now exposed at the surface. The Garleton Hills north of Haddington, and the Braid Hills and Blackford Hill are formed from more extensive spreads of lavas.

Many of these hills, which add variety to the lowlands, have had their western faces sharpened by glacial erosion while their eastern slopes, relatively protected from glacial scouring, are more gentle, with tails of sedimentary rock and unconsolidated deposits in the lee of the ice flow. This kind of landform is known as a 'crag and tail'. The Castle Rock of Edinburgh is the classic example but similar landforms can be seen on Calton Hill, North Berwick Law, and Traprain Law.

Similar volcanic hills are a feature of the central Tweed valley. The

Plate 1 Arthur's Seat and Salisbury Crags, Edinburgh. The remains of an ancient eroded volcano dominate the city centre

most striking examples are the Eildon Hills which rise above the Tweed valley at Melrose. They are the remnants of a huge laccolith which was intruded into the surrounding sediments. Other rocky hills of basalt and agglomerate, like Rubers Law, and Dunion, mark the last remnants of ancient volcanoes, or are igneous intrusions like Dirrington Law. In the past these rocky hills, in the Lothians and the Merse, were prime sites for fortifications.

The Merse, the plain of the lower Tweed, like the Lothians is a structural basin dipping towards the sea with older rocks around the rim and younger ones in the centre. Much of the Merse is underlain by sandstones from Old Red Sandstone and Carboniferous times. Although Carboniferous limestones outcrop near the coast there are no coal measures. As a result the Merse has remained purely agricultural while the Lothians have been strongly affected by industrial activity based on coal mining.

The Midlothian coalfield and the shallow coal basin which extends into East Lothian contain the greatest fuel reserves. In the past only the shallower Upper Coals were mined, and the steeply-dipping seams of the Lower Coals where they outcropped around the edges of the basin, but modern collieries like Bilston and Monktonhall work the deep seams of the Lower Coals in the centre of the basin. Coal that occurred close to the surface was worked from medieval times. Seams also outcropped along the coast, particularly around Prestonpans and Bo'ness; these districts were major exporters of coal as early as the seventeenth century. The smaller fragments of coal which were not worth shipping were burnt to evaporate seawater and produce sea salt. The Carboniferous strata have not resisted erosion very effectively and tend to form low ground. The beds of Carboniferous Limestone are much thinner than in Northern England and do not form 'karst' landscapes with the typical limestone pavements, scars and cave systems. In West Lothian the coal seams are thinner but the widespread Lower Carboniferous sandstones contain oil shales which were mined in the later nineteenth century giving rise to a major industry whose distinctive imprint is still evident in the landscape.

THE LEGACY OF THE ICE AGE

During the Ice Age the entire area was overwhelmed by an ice sheet. Apart from eroding the volcanic hills into crag and tail features the effects of the ice in the lowlands were mainly depositional. The ice sheet plastered a thick layer of till, a deposit of stones and boulders in a dense clayey matrix, over much of the area. The till was produced from the ground-down remains of rocks carried by the ice. In places the till was sculptured into elongated rounded hills called drumlins, often a kilometre (0.6 mile) long and up to 30m (100ft) high. These drumlins, aligned parallel to the direction of ice flow, form a huge 'swarm' in the lower Tweed valley from south of the Eildon Hills to the outskirts of Berwick. Here they have had a profound influence on settlement. Villages like Swinton and Smail-holm are located on the well-drained crests of drumlins while the hollows between were marshy and ill-drained in the past and sometimes remain so today. Major roads tend to follow the grain of the drumlin country, while minor roads cut between the oval hills at right angles producing a grid pattern.

The landscape was also influenced by meltwater streams which flowed away from the ice sheets. As the ice became thinner and melted, hills like the Pentlands and the Lammermuirs began to emerge above the ice while the adjoining lowlands were still buried. Meltwater flowing along or just under the margins of the ice carved channels against the hillsides. Sometimes these are minor features but where meltwater was able to erode along geological faults, some striking landforms were produced. A 30km (20 mile) belt of country

Plate 2 A complex set of glacial meltwater channels on the edge of the Pentland Hills near Carlops

around the Lammermuirs from near Gifford almost to St Abb's Head is dissected by a series of these channels. Some are up to 60m (200ft) deep. The eastern edge of the Pentlands between Carlops and Dolphinton has an equally impressive set of channels, the deepest of which are cut along the line of the Pentland Fault. The Windy Gowl, in which the village of Carlops sits, is one of the largest. North of Carlops the meltwater channel has been occupied in post-glacial times by the river North Esk but the splendid gorge between Carlops and Penicuik was cut by glacial meltwater rather than the modern stream.

As the thickness of the ice decreased channels were cut at lower and lower levels until even the northern slopes of the Garleton Hills were dissected by meltwater channels. The streams which emerged from under the retreating ice sheets were heavily laden with sediment and this was deposited as huge fans of sand and gravel around the ice margins. Sometimes these sheets of debris were sculptured into ridges (kames) and hollows (kettle holes) where the material was washed up against blocks of abandoned or 'dead' ice which subsequently melted. Elsewhere rivers flowing under the ice deposited gravels in the floors of ice-walled tunnels leaving sinuous ridges, or eskers, when the ice finally melted. Good examples can be seen between West Linton and Dolphinton. It is interesting to note that north of Greenlaw one esker is so prominent and so apparently artificial that it is still marked on the Ordnance Survey map as an antiquity!

The disappearance of the ice sheets also produced changes in sea level. At the end of the Ice Age, sea level was higher relative to the land than at present. This was because large quantities of water were being released from the melting ice at a time when the land, which had been depressed by the weight of the ice, had not begun to recover. These high late-glacial seas cut a series of cliffs and platforms up to 35m (115ft) above present sea level. Between Port Seton and Aberlady the old cliffline, now over 1km (0.6 mile) from the sea, can be traced as a step in the landscape.

High late-glacial seas also deposited beach material. Raised beaches can be traced near Hopetoun House, from Cramond almost to North Berwick, and around Dunbar. Sea level gradually fell with the recovery of the land from the weight of ice but at the end of the Ice Age sea level was higher again for a period around 7,500–6,500 years ago when the rapid decay of the North American and Scandinavian ice sheets returned vast quantities of water to the oceans. This phase of high sea level produced the 'main postglacial' shoreline at altitudes ranging from around 9m (30ft) above present sea level at the mouth of the Water of Leith to about 6m (20ft) around the Tyne estuary. Large parts of northern Edinburgh are built on this raised beach. Near Aberlady marine clays were laid down as mudflats which were later to form some of the richest soils in the Lothians. These raised beaches were often attractive for early settlement because of their well-drained, easily worked soils.

THE SPREAD OF THE WILDWOOD

As the climate warmed, the bare tundra landscape which had developed in the wake of the retreating ice was gradually replaced by woodland. At first only hardy birch and hazel spread northwards. As conditions became warmer, they were followed by oak, ash and elm, with alder in wetter locations. By around 6–7,000 years ago a full woodland cover had developed over most of the area. The treeline during this moist, mild climatic phase may have been as high as 800m (2,625ft). Only the most marshy areas, exposed coastal sites, and the highest hills were not forested although in the wetter conditions around 7,000 years ago peat was starting to form in more poorly drained areas.

We do not know a great deal about the composition of the wildwood of south-east Scotland before the advent of man for little research has been carried out on the fossil pollen deposits in lake sediments and peat bogs, which provide a good picture of the vegetation cover in the early postglacial period. Rather than a uniform mixed oak woodland it is probably more accurate to visualise a complex mosaic of woodland types influenced by local variations in soils, slope, drainage, and other factors. At its upper levels, the oak-dominated woodland probably gave way to a more open birch scrub. The forests were inhabited by a range of animals, including elk, wild horse, wild ox, beaver, wild boar, wolf and brown bear; sadly, all these magnificent animals have long since been eliminated by man.

Into this forested landscape early man arrived some 9,000 years ago. Over succeeding millennia he modified it increasingly by clearance, burning and the effects of his livestock which nibbled young saplings and prevented cleared areas from reverting to woodland. The clearance of the woodland led to erosion of exposed soils, and the accelerated leaching of their nutrients. This made them increasingly acid and impoverished, encouraging the formation of peat which in many areas may have been as much the result of man as of a wetter climate. The acid grasslands and heather moors which cover the hills today are a purely artificial creation. Attractive to some people, bleak and empty to others, they are a ravaged landscape caused by the deterioration of the environment following woodland clearance.

Although the chronology of man's attack on the wildwood has been established in detail for many parts of Britain we know only the outlines of the process in this area. Indications are that the first scattered hunters and gatherers had little impact on the woodlands. The arrival of the first farming communities began the long process of clearing the woodlands. From around 3000BC there are indications of a drop in the proportion of tree pollen from sites in southern Scotland and a corresponding increase in the pollen of grasses and flowering plants. This suggests that man was starting to clear areas of woodland for pasture and for raising crops. At first the clearings were small and only temporary but the scale of deforestation increased as the population rose from the Bronze Age into the Iron Age. There is evidence that timber supplies may have been running out around some settlements by the later Iron Age but the Romans do not seem to have experienced undue difficulty in obtaining timber to build their forts. It is likely that there were still extensive areas of woodland left in early historic times.

2
LANDSCAPE
BEFORE HISTORY

SOUTH-EAST Scotland was inhabited for several thousand years before the first documentary sources begin to tell us something about the landscape and the people who shaped it. Thus for most of the period in which man has been active in this area we can reconstruct the landscape only by using archaeological evidence. This involves the study of surface remains in the field, the identification of crop mark sites from aerial photographs and the interpretation of excavated structures and artefacts. The extent of our knowledge, particularly for early millennia, is still limited. Even for later prehistory there is much debate and little certainty concerning the nature and patterns of human activity.

A problem in understanding how prehistoric man shaped, and was influenced by, his environment is that remains of settlements and other sites occur mainly in the uplands. Throughout the lowlands intensive exploitation of the land, particularly deep ploughing in the last two centuries, has obliterated most earlier features. In more marginal areas, where the ground has been less disturbed in later times, traces of prehistoric man are more abundant. Archaeologists once considered that this represented the actual distribution of early human activity, arguing that man did not have the ability to clear the dense woodlands of the lowlands nor the technology to cultivate their heavy clay soils. However, stray artefacts turned up by the plough suggest that man was indeed active in the lowlands. Moreover, in recent years aerial surveys have begun to show up many prehistoric sites in the lowlands whose surface traces have been totally obliterated by later agriculture.

THE FIRST SETTLERS: MYSTERY, RITUAL AND DEATH

It is likely that the first bands of hunters moved into this area up the east coast some 9,000 years ago. The only evidence of their activity in the lowlands is the discovery of shell middens and finds of flint tools along the coast at sites like Inveravon and Hedderwick, and implements found on inland hills like Traprain Law and Arthur's Seat. Scatters of flint and chert tools have also been found along the valleys of the Tweed and its tributaries and in the Biggar area on the important routeway from the Tweed to the Clyde. These finds appear to date from the fifth or fourth millennium BC and may be the remains of temporary summer camps established by coastal dwellers exploiting the inland resources of river and forest.

From about 3500BC a new wave of immigrants arrived, bringing domesticated animals and the knowledge of agriculture. Remains of these first farming communities are a little more abundant than those of their hunter/gatherer predecessors. A few examples of the type of burial monument known as long cairns occur, like the Mutiny Stones near Longformacus and one on the edge of the Pentlands near Dolphinton. Some have remains of cists or chambers as at Long Knowe in Roxburghshire and may be related to the chambered tombs of south-west Scotland and the Firth of Clyde. Other burial mounds, built mainly of earth, may be linked with the long barrows of southern England. The high altitudes at which some of these features occur may indicate that the earliest farmers started the attack on the woodlands from their upper edge where the trees were smaller and more scattered, only gradually moving downwards into the valleys.

The settlements of these first agriculturalists have still to be identified. Their houses were probably timber-built leaving no visible trace on the surface. Many sites may have been obliterated by later erosion. This makes it difficult to determine the function of a site at Meldon Bridge (205404), west of Peebles, dating from around 2300BC and unique in Scotland. Crop marks on aerial photographs revealed that a line of pits had been dug, cutting off a promontory between the Lyne Water and the Meldon Burn. Excavation showed that the pits had been used for bedding a series of timber posts forming a massive wooden barrier some 0.5km long. The remaining perimeter of the site was protected by the two streams. This barrier would have been quite a feat of construction at any date but is particularly impressive from this early period for it forms the first known timber defences in Britain. What did the barrier protect? Excavation of parts of the interior has provided evidence of burials and domestic occupation but the nature of the site remains uncertain. Given that such a massive timber barrier has left only the faintest of traces there may be many similar sites awaiting discovery.

By 2000BC further immigrants had arrived bringing the techniques

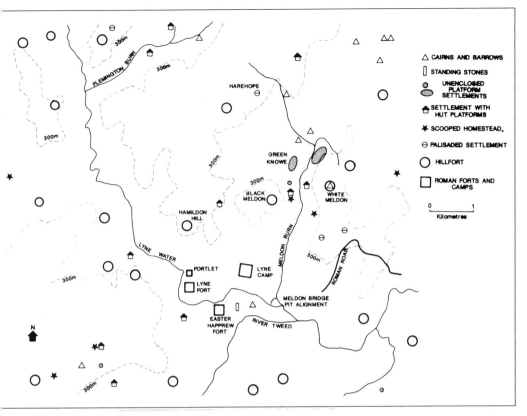

Fig 3 Prehistoric and Roman sites in the Meldon Bridge area

of smelting copper and casting bronze. Remains from the Bronze Age, though still enigmatic, are more abundant in the landscape, implying a larger population. The overall distribution of sites and stray finds suggests widespread occupation of the lowlands and major river valleys with a preference for lighter, more easily worked soils on raised beaches and the sands and gravels deposited by glacial meltwater. Unfortunately we know less about life in the Bronze Age than we do about death. Midden material and scatters of pottery at coastal locations like Gullane, North Berwick and Dunbar hint at the former existence of settlement sites but these have yet to be found. Most of the remains from this period are connected with burial or ritual. The new immigrants may have introduced new burial rites. There was a change from the Neolithic tradition of collective burial in long cairns and barrows, probably of only a minority of the population, to individual interments in stone-lined cists or cremations. Cist burials were often made without any surface feature to mark the site but sometimes small cairns of stones or earthen barrows were built over the graves.

On a grander scale were the larger burial cairns, perhaps of notable tribal leaders. These are often sited on exposed ridges or summits from which they would have been readily visible by the inhabitants of the surrounding lowlands. Two examples in the Pentlands, on Carnethy and East Cairn Hill, can be seen for miles. Similar ones occur in the Lammermuirs on Spartleton Edge (653656) and Priestlaw Hill (652624) while one on White Meldon overlooks the Tweed valley above Peebles. Other cairns occupy less elevated sites. An interesting group occurs between West Linton and Dolphinton on the eastern edge of the Pentlands. There are nine large cairns; the biggest, over 15m (49ft) diameter and nearly 4m (13ft) high, is particularly impressive. This group and other cairns in the area mark an ancient route from the Clyde valley to the Forth. It is likely that both the smaller cairns and barrows, and the larger hilltop cairns, date from early in the second millennium BC.

Ritual sites include henges, stone circles and standing stones. A henge monument, a circular bank enclosing a ceremonial area, has been discovered from aerial photographs near Overhowden at the head of Lauderdale (486552) but there is little to see on the ground. There are around a dozen stone circles in the area but they are less impressive than those in other parts of Britain. Many have been damaged so that only two or three stones of the original circle remain while others have been removed entirely in the course of later agricultural improvement. One circle survives at Kingside Hill (627650) in the Lammermuirs. It is a setting of thirty small stones in a circle with a diameter of about 12m (39ft). None of the stones is over 0.5m (19in) high. Inside is a low mound with a boulder on top, probably a burial cairn. The survival of other stone circles and burial cairns around the headwaters of the Whiteadder suggests that this was an important area for early settlement, perhaps at the uphill margins of the forest where the woodland was thinner and the trees easier to clear.

The function of isolated standing stones is even more obscure. There are around eighty in the area and there must once have been many more. Were they route or boundary markers, meeting places, monuments or memorial stones? Did they have some ritual or astronomical significance? Some have enigmatic carvings consisting of hollows, sometimes surrounded by circles, known as 'cup and ring' marks. Examples can be seen on a stone in the churchyard at Glencorse. The areas around standing stones have rarely been excavated but they do not always seem to have been linked to burials. Sometimes two or three standing stones occur close to burial cairns which may have been contemporary, as at Sheriff Muir

Plate 3 A standing stone near Biel, East Lothian, isolated and out of context in the middle of a landscape of agricultural improvement

(201402) or near Tweedsmuir (095239). In lowland areas many stones may have been moved with agricultural improvement from the late eighteenth century onwards. Even in intensively cultivated areas some have survived though, like the one at Easter Broomhouse (680766) which is marked by grooves cut by the winch cable of a nineteenth-century steam plough. Others have been moved from the centres of fields to their boundaries, like one built into a wall just north of Kirkton Manor near Peebles (228387).

The most complex and fascinating site from Neolithic and Bronze Age times is at Cairnpapple Hill, on a commanding viewpoint in the Bathgate Hills south of Linlithgow, where excavation has revealed a long sequence of ritual and burial activity from c2800BC to c500BC. The monument has been carefully preserved and is one of the most interesting early prehistoric sites in south-east Scotland. The first phase of development consisted of a series of cremation pits. This cemetery was then enclosed by an oval ditch and outer bank forming a henge measuring about 40 × 30m (131 × 98ft) with a setting of twenty-four standing stones which were removed in a later period of activity. This was followed by the building of a burial cairn about 15m (49ft) in diameter which was later enlarged to 30m (98ft). We can only guess at the kinds of beliefs and rites associated with this long sequence of structures.

SETTLEMENT IN THE UPLANDS

We know little about how people lived and worked during the Bronze Age. It seems clear, however, that unenclosed clusters of round timber houses were normal during the second and earlier part of the first millennium BC. One type of settlement which is fairly easily recognisable consists of a number of circular or oval platforms up to 12–15m (40–50ft) in diameter, ranging from only one to a dozen or so strung out along a hillside or in tiers. Excavated material from the back of the slope was spread out downhill to form level foundations for timber huts. A site of this type has been excavated at Green Knowe (212434) near Peebles. Nine platforms have survived and there may once have been more. Adjoining them is an area of small cairns and low stone banks covering some 2.5ha (6.2 acres) today but probably once more extensive. These possibly represent stones cleared from small cultivation plots worked by the inhabitants of the settlement. On the opposite side of the valley a larger site with at least eighteen platforms can be seen. Excavation of one platform at Green Knowe showed that three successive round timber houses with wattle and daub walls had stood on it. Occupation appeared to have been intermittent and there was no reason to assume that all the platforms were necessarily in use at any one time.

Unenclosed platform settlements are most frequent in the upper Tweed valley at altitudes of around 275–305m (900–1,000ft) on south-facing slopes. They are rarely found at lower levels. This may be because on less steeply sloping ground the construction of platforms was unnecessary and the hut foundations have left no trace in the landscape. Nor is it clear whether such sites were permanently occupied or whether they were transhumance sites, the Bronze Age equivalent of medieval shielings.

Radiocarbon dates for Green Knowe indicated that the earliest period of occupation was around 1500BC. However, there is no reason why this site should have the oldest platforms in existence! The construction of settlements of this type can reasonably be extended back to around 1750BC while it is also probable that some continued to be used down to the middle of the first millennium BC. Even pushing back the earliest construction of these platforms as far as the evidence currently warrants there is still a gap of around 1000 years between the timber barrier at Meldon Bridge and the nearby Green Knowe platforms. It may be that excavation of other sites will provide evidence for the occupation of platforms at earlier dates but at the moment the nature of settlement in this area before the early second millennium remains a mystery. Many remains of habitations and cultivation plots may lie below the peat cover which developed over gentle hillslopes during the cooler, wetter conditions of later prehistoric times.

Unenclosed platform sites seem to represent the maximum penetration of settlement into the uplands during the comparatively warm and dry Bronze Age. In the upper Tweed area they occur 5km (3 miles) further up the main valley than the highest known palisaded settlements, which are believed to be later in date, and 9km (5.6 miles) higher than Iron Age hillforts or Romano-British settlements. A similar pattern, over shorter distances, is evident in the Cheviots. Elsewhere in upland Britain it has been suggested that an ecological crisis caused by extensive woodland clearance and over-cultivation led to soil exhaustion and widespread erosion. This, with the onset of cooler and wetter climatic conditions, may have encouraged the abandonment of higher, more exposed sites.

FORTS AND FRONTIERS

Apart from the Neolithic site at Meldon Bridge, settlements from before the Iron Age are open and undefended. During the Iron Age, however, there was a marked trend towards constructing defences around settlements which, moreover, were often located on less accessible hilltops and ridges. It has been suggested that a gradual filling up of the landscape with continued population growth may have caused communities to come into increasing competition and even conflict over resources like timber and pasture. Whatever the reason it became necessary to protect settlements, and possibly also livestock, behind increasingly massive and sophisticated defences. A deteriorating climate with wetter and cooler conditions may have hastened this process. If the new techniques of iron working were introduced by immigrant Celtic peoples this too may have caused friction and increased the need for defence.

The earliest defences were simple wooden stockades with upright timbers set in a bedding trench. These palisaded sites began to appear early in the first millennium BC. Sometimes there were two concentric rings of posts with enough space between corralling livestock. The largest sites of this type, like White Hill (478057) and Hayhope Knowe (860176), enclosed some 2ha (5 acres) and contained up to fifteen huts suggesting that they were small villages but many with only two or three huts were clearly inhabited by single families. The entrance of a double palisaded settlement at Harehope (196445) was closed by timber gates and flanked by watchtowers.

Palisaded sites remained in use for a long period; from at least 700BC into the Christian era. The earlier ones overlapped with unenclosed platform settlements. There was no overnight transformation from open communities to defended ones. On around a dozen sites excavations have shown that palisades were erected around previously open settlements and that, at a later date, they were replaced by more substantial ramparts and ditches. This was the pattern at Hownam Rings (791194) which was excavated in the late 1940s. This excavation established a chronology of house and settlement types for the Iron Age in this area which still forms a basis for interpretation although some modifications have been made to it. A similar evolutionary sequence was found recently at Broxmouth near Dunbar. This sequence was not universal though. Not all palisaded settlements developed into hillforts and where this did happen the transition was not necessarily simultaneous at different sites.

The most impressive landscape features from late prehistoric times in south-east Scotland are hillforts. The term is misleading on two counts. First, not all fortified sites were located on hilltops. One of 'the most notable forts in the Lothians, the Chesters, near Drem, is sited on low ground at the foot of the Garleton Hills and is closely overlooked by a ridge. Possibly the ramparts here were designed more for prestige than utility. The discovery of crop-mark sites, like the fort at Broxmouth which was situated only 25m (82ft) above sea level, shows that such sites were built on the coastal plain and could be almost completely obliterated by later cultivation.

The term 'fort' also implies a purely military function. In fact most sites designated 'forts' were defended hamlets or villages. There was a range of settlements from a few large forts down to large numbers of small enclosed farms. Many forts enclosed areas of around 0.3ha (0.75 acres). The smaller forts were probably equivalent to medieval tower houses or moated sites; places which were essentially farms but which could be defended at need. It has been suggested for sites like Broxmouth that the amount of labour required to construct their ramparts and the manpower needed to defend their perimeters were disproportionate to the small numbers of huts protected. This may imply that they were refuges for people living in surrounding, undefended settlements, a class of site which has yet to be discovered but which by its nature would leave little trace.

On a number of sites a progression from a wooden palisade to a thick stone wall and then multiple earthen ramparts and ditches has been noted. This sequence may indicate that timber was becoming scarce, at least adjacent to the settlements, so that fort-builders turned increasingly to stone and earth. It has been calculated that a wooden palisade would have used the timber from 1–2ha (2.5–5 acres) of forest and would have needed replacing every fifteen to twenty years, not to mention the timber for the huts inside the defences. However, the Iron Age landscape had not been completely stripped of woodland because trees were available for the timber lacing which was sometimes used to stabilise stone walls and earth ramparts which were presumably topped by wooden palisades as well. In some cases, as at Tinnis Castle upstream from Peebles, the timbers had been set alight, whether by accident or enemy action is uncertain, and the heat had vitrified the stonework.

The change from single stone walls to multiple earth ramparts was not universal. However, the transition was widespread and there may have been military reasons for it. One possibility is the development of sling warfare. In defending a fort using close-range weapons like spears and swords the ideal tactic was to trap attackers in the ditch immediately below a single steep-faced rampart on which the defenders were massed. Slings, by contrast, were long-distance weapons and required a different style of defence. Outer ramparts were needed to protect the slingers from close-range weapons. The slingers themselves needed a high inner rampart from which they could launch their stones. In the later part of the period chariot warfare probably developed too. Some forts have defences which were designed to keep charioteers or other attackers even further from the ramparts. Around the forts on Cademuir Hill and Dreva in Tweeddale and Kames Hill near Edinburgh are areas protected by *chevaux de frise*, closely set pointed stones set upright in the ground. They were designed to stop chariots and impede cavalry or foot soldiers. In the Cheviots many forts, like the one on Woden Law, were protected by outlying dykes blocking the gently-sloping crests of ridges and ending where the slope steepens on each side. In some cases these may have been designed for corralling livestock, or keeping animals away from cultivated ground, but in others they appear to be outer defences, perhaps against chariots.

Although most forts enclose only limited areas a few are much bigger and may have been tribal capitals like the fort on Traprain Law in East Lothian. Traprain Law is a steep sided, whale-backed hill which can be seen from a long distance away. The fort on it must have been an imposing symbol of authority. It was excavated early in the present century and although the excavations were not as sophisticated as modern ones they provided an outline of the development of the site. The ramparts, at their maximum, defended an area of 17ha (42 acres). The fort began in late Bronze Age times with a rampart enclosing only 4ha (10 acres). A more extensive stone rampart was built about 700BC taking in an area twice as large. Around the first century AD the lower western slopes of the hill were brought within the defences and the settlement reached its maximum size about AD300. At its peak Traprain was densely built up with houses laid out around courtyards and streets. The fort may have been the capital of a tribe known to the Romans as the Votadini whose territory seems to have encompassed much of the Lothians and the Merse.

In late Iron Age times the central and upper Tweed valley was occupied by a people whom the Romans called the Selgovae. Their capital was the great fort on Eildon Hill North. The multiple ramparts on Eildon Hill North enclose an area roughly equal to Traprain and the fort grew in a similar way from a small original core. The ramparts of the last phase form three concentric lines but in many places they appear as terraces rather than upstanding features. The terraces may have been cut into the hillside to provide foundations on which the ramparts were raised. The ramparts themselves may have been eroded, or possibly deliberately levelled by the Romans. Within the defences nearly 300 hut platforms have been identified and others have probably been destroyed by a plantation on the south side of the hill. If a substantial proportion of the huts was occupied simultaneously the fort may have had a population of over 1,000.

Within palisaded enclosures and forts, foundations of huts can often be seen as circular grooves in the ground, levelled platforms cut into the slope, or stone foundations. Archaeologists have worked out a sequence of hut development but this is rarely apparent from the surface remains. The term 'hut' is almost as much of a misnomer as 'fort' carrying implications of small size and squalor. It is difficult to accept that people who could defend themselves so effectively could not build comfortable weathertight homes and the floorspace of many of the huts is considerable. Some of them may have been used for wintering livestock; up to thirty cattle could have been accommodated in the largest ones.

THE COMING OF THE ROMANS

The Roman occupation of southern Scotland was a series of brief interludes. It was largely military in character and evidence of civilian settlement is scanty. Traces of a *vicus*, or civil settlement, have been discovered outside the fort at Inveresk. Excavations have uncovered traces of stone and timber houses, some with hypocaust systems, and cobbled streets leading towards the fort. Inveresk is the nearest thing to a Roman town in this area. Aerial photographs have revealed traces of an extensive system of rectangular fields beyond the *vicus*. There may have been a similar civilian settlement with its fields adjoining the Antonine fort at Carriden. Before the discovery of these field systems it might have been concluded that the Roman impact on the landscape of southern Scotland was limited. This interpretation may need revising.

In terms of what is visible on the ground the Roman legacy is not impressive: a handful of forts, a few signal stations, and some sections of road, along with a much larger number of contemporary native sites. Nevertheless, because Roman remains are so distinctive, reflecting the contrast between the efficient organisation of Imperial Rome and the less advanced tribes which they conquered, and because they can be tied, however vaguely, into an historical chronology, the Roman legacy in the landscape is particularly fascinating.

Roman involvement in this area began with the campaigns of Agricola in AD80. He established the basic network of roads and military sites in southern Scotland. His strategy seems to have involved a pincer movement with two forces, one crossing the Cheviots to the Eildon Hills then moving up Lauderdale, the other marching through Clydesdale and the eastern side of the Pentlands. These manoeuvres may have been designed to isolate the warlike Selgovae. The lines of march of Agricola's legions were marked by temporary camps and later by roads with chains of permanent forts. The routes chosen by Agricola during this first campaign dictated the pattern of Roman activity throughout their occupation.

31

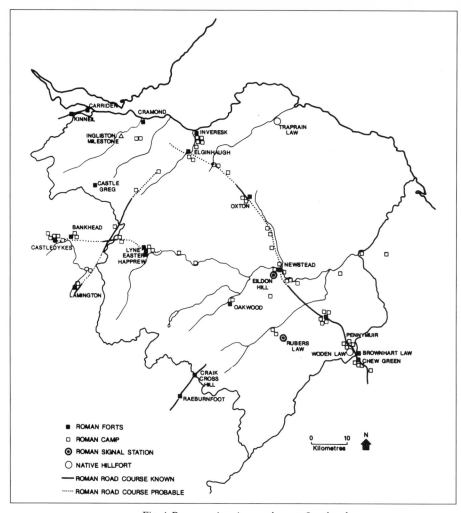

Fig 4 Roman sites in south-east Scotland

In AD84 Agricola defeated the Caledonians at Mons Graupius, somewhere in north-east Scotland and all the country south of the Grampians came under Roman control. Around AD90, however, the need to transfer troops to the Danube frontier caused the Romans to pull back, establishing a line of forts between the Forth and Clyde and strengthening some of the forts in southern Scotland, particularly Newstead, near Melrose. Newstead became the centre of operations for south-east Scotland accommodating a battle group of legionaries and mounted auxiliaries, an unusual but flexible arrangement. The natives seem to have taken the offensive thereafter and there is evidence of the violent destruction of forts as far south as the Tyne after about AD98, followed by a Roman counter-attack. Newstead and other forts north of the Cheviots were abandoned

32

around AD105, possibly when more troops were withdrawn, and the frontier was established along Hadrian's Wall in the 120s.

In 138–9 the Romans advanced into Scotland again and established a new frontier, the Antonine Wall, between the Forth and Clyde estuaries. A few years later a rebellion of the Brigantes in Northern England caused it and other forts to be evacuated. There is evidence of destruction at Newstead but whether due to enemy action or a deliberate dismantling of the defences by the Romans is not clear. Around 159 the Antonine Wall was re-garrisoned and seems to have been held till 184 when the natives broke through. The wall was abandoned and the frontier was fixed along Hadrian's Wall once more. In AD208 the Emperor Septimus Severus led a major expedition into Scotland during which bases like Cramond were re-fortified but the Roman presence was short-lived. Following the death of Severus, his son Caracalla concluded a treaty with the tribes north of the Forth and withdrew once more.

Fig 4 shows the known network of Roman roads and forts in south-east Scotland. There are no sites east of Dere Street in the area inhabited by the Votadini and it has been supposed from this that their relations with the Romans were peaceful. The Romans allowed them to maintain the defences of their capital on Traprain Law. The Selgovae in the central and upper Tweed valley seem to have been more troublesome. The defences of their capital on Eildon Hill North were dismantled, as were the ramparts of other large forts in this area. It cannot have been a coincidence that the Romans built their most powerful fort at Newstead immediately below the Eildon Hills.

ROMAN CAMPS AND FORTS

Because their forts were built on low ground, trusting to the quality of their defences and the discipline of their defenders rather than inaccessibility, many have been obliterated. Of Newstead, the key centre for the whole region, defended by massive earth ramparts and ditches, not a vestige remains on the surface. Excavation has established a complex sequence of building starting with two temporary camps, continuing with the Agricolan fort, which was defended by a rampart of beaten clay 7m (23ft) thick and a double ditch, and followed by three later phases of rebuilding.

There is also nothing to see at Inveresk, where a church and the suburbs of Musselburgh have spread over the site. At Cramond, another Roman port which may have been used to supply the garrisons on the Antonine Wall, the foundations of some of the buildings are marked out in the churchyard. A short way along the coast, on the far side of the River Almond, is an isolated outcrop called Eagle Rock (184774). On one side is a badly worn sculpture formerly thought to be a Roman eagle but now interpreted as a figure of Mercury.

Other sites undoubtedly await discovery. Aerial surveys during the 1970s and 1980s led to the identification of a number of previously unrecorded temporary camps which show up as crop marks only in particularly dry years. Because of the rather random way that such sites are revealed it can be confidently predicted that more will eventually be located. Fig 4 shows these recently discovered sites, along with others which were plotted by antiquarians as long ago as the eighteenth century. Attempts have been made to distinguish and date the camps on the basis of their size and shape and to relate them to specific campaigns. This does not always work but there are good grounds for believing that certain camps with distinctive entrances protected by outer traverses relate to the Agricolan campaigns.

One of the most interesting of these has been located at Woodhead (384639) on a promontory between the valley of the River Tyne and a tributary stream. The rectangular camp had attached to it a large polygonal annex which seemed to have been designed for storage rather than defence. It has been conjectured that this camp, close to the line of Dere Street, might have been established to exploit a particular resource. No convincing remains of Roman stone-quarrying have been found here and the most likely explanation is that the camp was set up for squads of troops to fell timber for the construction of a fort, perhaps sited somewhere near Pathhead. Other camps, with areas of up to 66ha (165 acres), large enough to accommodate an entire Roman army, have been linked to the later Severan campaigns. A line of them had been identified along Dere Street from Newstead to Inveresk at intervals of just over 11km (7 miles). One can visualise them as the relatively closely-spaced stopping places of a slowly-moving and ponderous Roman battle group.

Permanent forts may also await discovery. They were fairly regularly spaced along the main roads, and on this basis there ought to have been one somewhere near Carlops, 19km (12 miles) south of Edinburgh. One was indeed identified by an eighteenth-century antiquarian but this may have been a temporary camp, now almost invisible at ground level, which was recently identified north of Carlops, underlying the Roman road and probably relating to Agricola's campaigns. A permanent fort in this area has yet to be located. There may also have been one on Dere Street near Pathhead. At nearby Crichton stones with characteristic Roman chisel marks were re-used in a *souterrain* but the whereabouts of the fort from which they were taken is uncertain.

That the landscape still holds surprises, despite over three centuries of careful searching, was demonstrated in 1979. Archaeologists were undertaking an aerial survey to try to locate the place where Dere Street was thought to have crossed the North Esk. A short section of the road was identified by parch marks in a field. Its line, projected in one direction, matched up with the modern A7 running into the southern suburbs of Edinburgh, almost certainly on the course of the Roman road. In the other direction further parch marks revealed a hitherto undiscovered fort at Elginhaugh (319671). An annex was attached to the fort and a bath house had stood nearby. The entire fort was excavated in 1986, a huge undertaking which has only been done twice before anywhere in the Roman Empire. The plans of the timber barrack blocks, granaries, headquarters and commander's house were clearly identifiable as was the layout of the defences. The fort had been established during the Flavian period, and was the forerunner of the second-century fort at Inveresk 5km (3 miles) away. It had probably been occupied for only a decade or so before being evacuated.

The main Roman road into south-east Scotland was Dere Street which follows a curving path down from the Cheviots at Chew Green and then strikes directly towards Newstead. Traces of the original road, much altered by traffic in post-Roman times, can be seen in the Cheviots. East of Jedburgh its line is preserved by sections of minor road and further north by the A68. Its course up the western side of Lauderdale is uncertain but it is well marked crossing the moors of Soutra at a height of nearly 400m (1300ft). Its line through the lowlands to the north was uncertain before the discovery of the fort at Elginhaugh.

The other main Roman road ran from Clydesdale along the eastern side of the Pentlands towards the Forth. A branch road linked it with Newstead through the heart of Selgovae territory. Parts of this branch road, little altered, can be walked immediately west of Peebles (225416). Another branch road ran from Annandale via Eskdale across the bleak hills of Eskdalemuir to the Borthwick Water, a tributary of the Teviot, and on towards Newstead. At its highest point, on Craik Cross Hill, at over 450m (1400ft), stood a lone signal station, surely one of the remotest postings in the entire Roman Empire.

The best preserved major fort is at Lyne (187405) on a plateau overlooking the Lyne Water west of Peebles. It appears to have been built around AD158 to replace the earlier Agricolan fort at Easter

Plate 4 The ramparts and ditches of the Roman fort at Lyne, near Peebles

Happrew on the opposite side of the valley. The ramparts and ditches are clearly defined around most of the fort's perimeter although no internal features can be seen at ground level. Another fort was built at Oakwood (425249) to command the valleys of the Ettrick and Yarrow Waters. The ramparts here are fainter than at Lyne but are still discernible, as at the small Agricolan fort at Cappuck (694213), halfway between the Cheviots and Newstead.

The great fort at Newstead has vanished but on top of Eildon Hill North traces of a circular ditch enclosing an area of around 11m (36ft) diameter are visible. This was the drainage ditch surrounding a Roman signal tower which could relay messages from Newstead to other forts and patrols over a wide area. Remains of a similar signal station can be seen on Rubers Law. On the moors to the west of the Pentlands stands a rectangular enclosure known as Castle Greg (050592). It is much smaller than the main Roman forts, merely an outpost. It may have been built along the line of a road, or perhaps only a projected road, running north of the Pentlands from Clydesdale to the road west of Edinburgh at the River Almond but no traces of such a road have so far been discovered.

One of the most fascinating Roman sites is at Woden Law in the Cheviots. Here Dere Street passes over the shoulder of a hill crowned with an Iron Age fort. Its defences seem to have been demolished, probably when the Romans first arrived, but they subsequently used the site to practise siege warfare. They dug a series of banks and ditches around the fort just out of range of missiles thrown from the ramparts. Flat platforms on the siegeworks may have been used for mounting catapults. Nearby at Pennymuir (7513–7514) is the best preserved series of Roman temporary camps in Scotland. Four separate camps can be distinguished, although parts of them have been obliterated by cultivation. They may have accommodated the troops who practised their siegecraft on Woden Law.

NATIVE SETTLEMENTS AND FIELD SYSTEMS

The inhabitants of this area during the Roman period and succeeding centuries were descendants of the Iron Age folk who had probably never lost their tribal structure under Roman rule. During the Roman occupation native settlements in the uplands, particularly in the territory of the Votadini, took the form of groups of round stone-walled houses on undefended sites, sometimes overlying the ramparts of disused forts. Good examples can be seen on Manor Water at 207367 and 203329. Commonly such sites had two or three huts within an enclosure facing on to sunken yards which may have been hollowed out by the prolonged trampling of livestock. Other sites with similar scooped yards but timber rather than stone buildings may be of comparable date though there are indications that on some sites timber houses predated stone ones, the transition occurring after the Romans had arrived. The change may reflect a growing shortage of timber but the precise period during which such settlements were in use is not certain. Excavated examples have produced Roman pottery. Some archaeologists consider that they were first built before the Romans arrived and some certainly continued in use after they left.

What of native settlement in the lowlands at this time? The evidence is slimmer as so much has been destroyed by nearly 2,000 years of cultivation. However, a number of crop mark sites consisting of square or rectangular ditched enclosures have been identified between the Forth and the Tweed. Comparable sites in Northumberland have been excavated and dated to the late first/early second century AD. They consisted of one or two yards inside the entrance of the enclosure with timber buildings towards the rear. They may be lowland counterparts of the upland stone house and scooped enclosure sites. Many more may yet be discovered in the Lothians and the Merse.

Few pre-Roman Iron Age sites have so far been associated with field systems. Until recently it was assumed that the economy of south-east Scotland during the Iron Age was mainly pastoral and that these 'Celtic cowboys', when they grew crops at all, used hoes and digging sticks rather than ploughs. As a result it was assumed that any traces of ridge cultivation caused by ploughing near Iron Age sites were medieval in date. This circular argument meant that no Iron Age field systems could be identified. Cultivation ridges and terraces do occur near a number of hillforts like Arbory Hill, Cademuir and Woden Law and may have been contemporary with them.

Field systems are more clearly associated with some Romano-British settlements. Three examples can be found in the upper Tweed area at Dreva, and at the heads of the Stanhope and Glenrath valleys, remote sites which have been little disturbed since then. The obvious conclusion is that such field systems must once have spread lower down the valleys but have been obliterated except for these isolated remnants. The field system at Glenrath (213328–228323) is the largest and best preserved, comprising some 14ha (35 acres) strung out for 1.5km (1 mile) along the bottom of a steep-sided valley between scree slopes and ground which has been cultivated in later times. A series of circular stone huts is linked by small rectangular enclosures delimited by stony banks, the foundations of walls, running downhill and steps, or lynchets, running across the slope. The plots are small – around 0.2ha (0.5 acre) – and may have been cultivated by hand rather than by plough. Different in character was a field system at Tamshiel Rig, now covered by forestry plantations, where longer fields, perhaps designed for plough cultivation, were defined by walls radiating from a settlement and surrounded by a perimeter dyke enclosing about 12ha (30 acres).

Traces of prehistoric field systems are also beginning to be discovered in lowland areas. At Eskbank near Dalkeith aerial photographs have revealed a set of pit alignments. Excavation indicated that these did not support timber posts like the Neolithic site at Meldon Bridge. The holes had merely been dug and left to fill naturally under the effects of wind and weather. A radiocarbon date of around 110BC was obtained for material from one of them. Similar lines of pits radiating out from the Chesters hillfort near Drem seem to have been contemporary with at least one phase of occupation of the site.

What were these curious features? The answer comes from sites like Marygoldhill in Berwickshire and Milkieston Rings north of Peebles where the land has been less disturbed subsequently. There similar lines of holes were dug to provide material for earthen banks which ran alongside. The pits at Eskbank and Drem were probably dug for the same purpose but the banks have been ploughed out. These boundaries may have delimited fields or in some cases the limits of farms. They may be mere fragments of a complex and developed landscape from Iron Age and Romano-British times. Other hints of this almost vanished landscape include an extensive field system covering some 130ha (320 acres), identified from aerial photographs, at Newton in Midlothian. Here, sets of field boundaries run north to south about 400m (1300ft) apart with some traces of cross boundaries.

THE ANGLIAN SETTLEMENT

From the seventh to the ninth centuries AD much of the area came under the influence of the expanding Anglian kingdom of Bernicia. The Angles began to put pressure on the kingdom of Gododdin, which had developed from the old tribal unit of the Votadini, during the early seventh century and in 638 the Anglian King Oswald captured the Castle Rock of Edinburgh, their capital. It was not until after the Battle of Carham in 1018 that the frontier between Scotland and England was finally pushed southwards again to the Tweed.

The nature of the Anglian penetration of south-east Scotland is unclear. Once it was believed to have involved dense settlement by large numbers of immigrants who displaced the native Britons. More recently it has been suggested that the invasion was a lower-key process, a takeover at the top by a small elite with their followers who took control of the local population and their lands with a minimum of disruption.

The Anglian occupation, whatever its character, can be traced in place names. Anglian names are scattered throughout the Merse. In the Lothians they are most frequent in East Lothian. In West Lothian they are decidedly sparse. They penetrate a little way up the valleys of the Tweed and its tributaries but are generally absent from the uplands. The earliest type of Anglian name is thought to incorporate the element 'ingas' (the place of the people of) with 'ham' (a village) as in Whittinghame (the settlement of Hvita's people). Later and more widely spread are names ending in -ham (a settlement) and -ington (the settlement of), as in Letham, Morham, Mersington or Haddington. Later still, and pushing furthest up the Tweed, are names incorporating 'wic' (a farm) like Dawyck and Hawick.

Some places bearing these names are insignificant today and some have disappeared entirely. However, a surprising number are villages and hamlets which became parish and estate centres in medieval

Plate 5 The linear earthwork called the Catrail near its terminus at Robert's Linn Bridge, south of Hawick. The bank and ditch descend the slope in the foreground and head towards the prominent hill, the Maiden Paps, which may have made a convenient sighting point for the builders

times. This may indicate that the Anglians took over and renamed many existing major settlements from which they could control the surrounding countryside. The distribution pattern and chronology of Anglian names suggests a gradual spread of influence but the fact that they are virtually absent from the uplands has caused some scholars to suggest that these areas remained under British control, the upland/lowland split perhaps reflecting not only a cultural contrast but also a difference between pastoral and arable farming systems.

It is perhaps in the context of such a division that we can interpret some Border earthworks including the Catrail. The Catrail is a linear bank and ditch which was clearly designed as a territorial or boundary marker as it is too slight to have been a defensive line. It runs for some 20km (12.5 miles) around the head of the Teviot and its tributaries (Fig 5). Gaps in it mostly correspond with streams forming natural boundaries. In other places sections have been obliterated by later cultivation. The Catrail appears to have been built in short sections, sometimes clumsily joined, by different groups of people. A similar earthwork, once thought to be the northern part of the Catrail but now considered to be a separate effort, is the 'Picts' Work Dyke' which can be traced for nearly 11km (7 miles) across the valleys of the Gala Water, Tweed and Ettrick. It is unwise to place too much faith in old maps and descriptions of these earthworks, for early antiquaries, and the Ordnance Survey, tended to apply the label 'Catrail' to any bank and ditch in this area, often including old field boundaries which are almost certainly from a different period and features like hollowed roads which were completely different in character.

Less convincing as a territorial boundary is another linear earthwork in Berwickshire. A bank and ditch running east-west for over a mile north of Greenlaw is marked by the Ordnance Survey as 'Heriot's Dyke'. Eighteenth-century antiquarians believed that it once ran for over 32km (20 miles) from the lowlands near the junction of the Tweed and Whiteadder towards the hills north-east of Lauderdale. Detailed examination shows that there are only two clear sections of dyke; the one at Greenlaw and another 11km (7 miles) away between the Blythe Water and the Brunta Burn, east of Lauder. However, both sections of dyke end against streams which continue the natural east-west line of a potential boundary (see Fig 6). The gap between Westruther and the Brunta Burn could be plausibly filled by suggesting that this was once densely wooded or marshy ground which formed a natural barrier. It is possible, by stretching the imagination even further to extend this line further

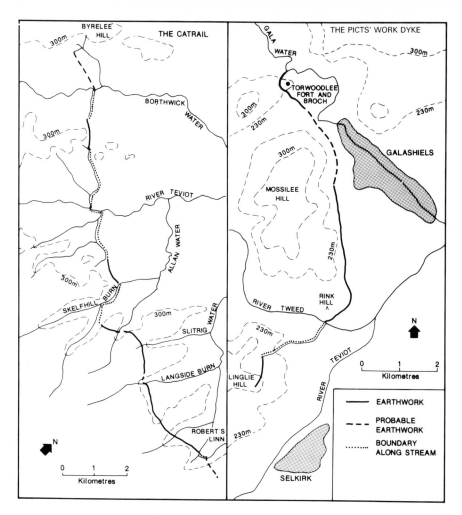

Fig 5 The Catrail and the Picts' Work Dyke

west to the head of Lauderdale by linking up a series of streams and cross-ridge dykes, and to the east by following the Blackadder Water downstream (Fig 6). The trouble is that you can always find bits of earthwork and suitably aligned streams to fit your theory no matter what direction you want to go, especially if you explain away awkward gaps as having been thickly forested! If these sections were once linked into a continuous boundary then they divided lowland from upland in a similar manner to the Catrail and the Picts' Work Dyke, the line of Heriot's Dyke north of Greenlaw merely straightening out an inconveniently aligned stretch of the Blackadder Water.

Although the Angles held this area for some 300 years their legacy in the landscape is elusive. On Doon Hill (686755), an outlier of the

42

Lammermuirs, aerial photography revealed remains which, when excavated, turned out to be two superimposed timber halls enclosed by polygonal wooden palisades. The later hall was similar to the seventh-century palace of King Oswy of Northumbria at Yeavering and must have been close to it in date. The earlier hall at Doon Hill, dating from the sixth century, had similar proportions but differed in its carpentry techniques with unusual V-shaped protruding gables which have not so far been matched elsewhere.

This first hall, which had been occupied for at least fifty years and perhaps as much as a century, seemed to reflect Anglian influences in design while preserving distinctive local building techniques. Perhaps it was built for a British tribal ruler. It was burnt down and the second, Anglian, hall built immediately after to replace it. Here we have evidence of a violent initial conquest followed by a takeover which emphasised continuity in the site and style of building and probably in the management of the lands around it. The foundations of the timber halls have been marked on the ground; until recently

Fig 6 Heriot's Dyke

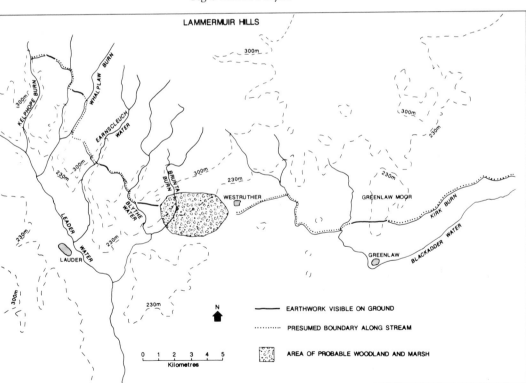

Plate 6 The coast at Dunbar. The upstanding pillars of rock are plugs of agglomerate in former volcanic vents

this was the only secular Anglian-period site to have been excavated in south-east Scotland. However, as this book was being written first reports appeared of the discovery of a new Dark Age site on the cliffs at Dunbar. It consisted of a large timber hall that may have belonged to King Ecgfrith of Northumbria or one of his administrators. Aerial photography has also revealed crop marks beside the Tweed near Sprouston which appear to be similar. Unfortunately they lie under top-quality arable land and are unlikely to be excavated!

The existing evidence relating to man and how he shaped the landscape of south-east Scotland during prehistoric and early historic times is likely to be extended in the future by new discoveries. As a result, interpretations may change significantly, as they have already done in the past. Partly for these reasons the landscape remains from these early times have a fascination all of their own.

3

FIELD AND FARM:
THE PRE-IMPROVEMENT
COUNTRYSIDE

T HE last chapter has shown that the legacy in the landscape from prehistoric times is much greater than many people would have supposed only a few years ago. In this chapter we shall see that the pre-improvement contribution is also considerable. Medieval castles and churches are considered separately in later chapters; here we will look at some of the less obvious features of the countryside from before the Agricultural Revolution.

VILLAGES AND *FERM TOUNS*

In the Lothians and the Merse, unlike other parts of Scotland, there can be found many villages whose origins go back to medieval times. In West Lothian industrial development has obscured this pattern of village settlement. Around Edinburgh former villages like Corstorphine and Duddingston have been absorbed by the growing suburbs of the city. East Lothian and the Merse are the areas in which this pattern of old villages is best preserved. There are settlements laid out around greens, focussing on the parish church, an old market cross or, sometimes, the gates of the local 'big house'.

Elsewhere in Scotland the normal settlement pattern before the eighteenth century was a dispersed one of farmsteads and cottages or small hamlets. Villages are generally of recent origin, planned foundations from the eighteenth and nineteenth centuries. The villages of south-east Scotland are different and have a good deal in common with settlements in Northumberland. This has prompted historians to look to the Anglian occupation between the seventh and ninth centuries AD at a time when such villages may have been established. If, however, as was suggested in the last chapter, this

45

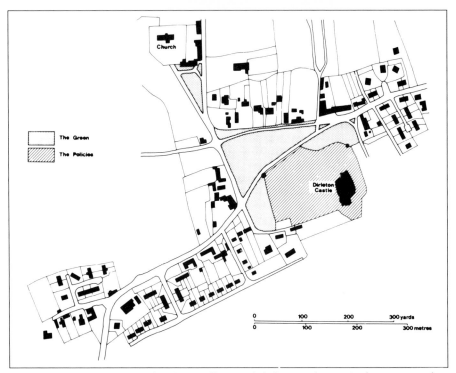

Fig 7 The present layout of Dirleton village and (below) its layout in the seventeenth century

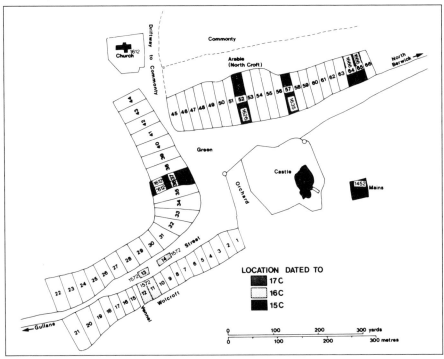

was less an invasion than a change in overlordship then we cannot visualise waves of migrants moving into the area and founding new village settlements; another explanation for the origin of these villages is necessary.

It is true that many villages in the Lothians and the Merse have Anglian names but this does not necessarily mean that the settlements, as villages, are as old as this. There is no evidence that the Anglian incomers favoured villages any more than the British inhabitants. It is impossible to show that the villages originated as early as this and the likelihood is that they developed at a later date. Many were village-sized by the fourteenth century to judge from surviving records but there is a gap of some 600 years between the Anglian settlement and these documents, a gap during which many changes may have occurred.

The plans of some villages, particularly those which focus on large greens like Denholm, Dirleton and Midlem, suggest links with north-eastern England where village greens are common. For some northern English villages the layout around a green has been shown to have originated during medieval times and it is possible that this was also the case in south-east Scotland. For Dirleton, estate papers show that its present layout existed in the late sixteenth century and was not the result of some comparatively modern estate-planning scheme (Fig 7). If this plan existed in the sixteenth century it might well go back to medieval times but this suggestion has yet to be confirmed. It may be no coincidence that many regularly-laid out villages with greens, like Ancrum, Bowden and Maxton in the Merse, were granted charters as market centres during the sixteenth or seventeenth centuries. It is possible that their layout was altered at this time to provide an open market place, the modern green.

Over much of the area, however, the pre-improvement settlement pattern was a dispersed one of small irregular hamlets or *ferm touns*, often representing a farm worked by a group of tenants. Parish churches provided a focus for slightly larger hamlets or *kirk touns*. Many *kirk touns* have changed their character, having been developed as market centres or estate villages but some, like Kirkton Manor, retain their original features. In such settlements you may find a pub and a post office as well as a church but rarely more in the way of services. A castle or mill was also a nucleating force and places with names containing 'castleton' or 'milton' are common. Most estates had their home farm or *mains*, another common place name. The *mains* was a survival from the medieval demesne lands which were under the feudal lord's own management, generally on the most fertile soils and adjacent to his castle or hall. By the seventeenth century many *mains* were leased to tenants but some were still worked by proprietors. In such cases landowners often retained the old feudal labour services and required their tenants to spend a certain number of days a year ploughing, harrowing and harvesting on the *mains*.

In periods of population growth, as in the sixteenth century, it was uncommon for *ferm touns* to grow into villages; there was generally not enough good-quality land near at hand to encourage this. Instead, townships were split so that on the modern map one often finds pairs or groups of farms with the same name differentiated by prefixes like Over, Mid and Nether, or Easter and Wester. The timing of this process of township splitting can frequently be roughly established from successive estate rentals. In Ettrick Forest a document of 1456 records the farm of Mountbenger but by 1500 it had been divided into Easter and Wester Mountbenger. In the same area the farms of Deloraine and Kershope were divided at a later date while the original settlement of Eldinhope developed into three farms called Over and Mid Eldinhope and Eldinhopeknowe.

Most *ferm touns* were transformed, between the seventeenth and nineteenth centuries, into the large single farmsteads which dominate the modern landscape. This was achieved gradually by the amalgamation and consolidation of holdings on the old group farms and their replacement by large units worked by a single tenant with the aid of hired labour. The *ferm touns* were mostly replaced by large farmsteads on the same or adjacent sites. If you compare any old estate rental with the modern Ordnance Survey map you will find that most pre-improvement farm names have survived. An interesting example of a *ferm toun* which remains little changed is Swanston on the southern outskirts of Edinburgh. Here the old cottages, thatched, whitewashed and possibly dating from the seventeenth century, are laid out around a small green, with a later school and farmstead. Although some later cottages with slate roofs have been added, the older buildings have escaped the hand of the improver. Making allowance for their neat and tidy modern appearance they

---

(*opposite above*) Crowned by a major Iron Age hillfort, the volcanic summits of the Eildon Hills dominate the central section of the Tweed valley (*BTA/ETB*)

(*below*) Tantallon Castle, the clifftop stronghold of the Douglas family with the Bass Rock, island fortress and prison in the background (*BTA/ETB*)

(*overleaf*) The royal palace of Linlithgow and the imposing burgh kirk seen from across Linlithgow Loch (*BTA/ETB*)

Tyninghame House, East Lothian, is a good example of nineteenth-century Scots baronial architecture *(BTA/ETB)*

give a good impression of what many *ferm touns* would have looked like before the later eighteenth century.

DESERTED SETTLEMENTS

In England, it has been said, you are rarely more than a few miles from the site of a deserted medieval village. Identifying, surveying and sometimes excavating such sites has become a major activity among local historians. In south-east Scotland the study of deserted settlements has not advanced as far for many reasons. First, there is less evidence of widespread settlement desertion and shrinkage in late-medieval times as occurred in parts of England. Some causes of desertion, such as the conversion of land from arable to sheep pasture and the replacement of whole communities by a single shepherd, did not apply in Scotland. It is also harder to identify deserted sites in the Lothians and the Merse, even compared with Northumberland where many abandoned villages are known. This appears to be due to the greater intensity with which the land has been worked on the Scottish side of the Border during the last three centuries. In addition in south-east Scotland settlements were small and their houses so flimsily built that they have left fewer traces in the landscape than the more substantial peasant houses of late-medieval England.

The fact that many villages in south-east Scotland have ancient place names demonstrates their durability through the centuries. Not all early villages have survived though. One deserted village whose site is marked on larger-scale Ordnance Survey maps is Morham in East Lothian (552722). The parish kirk still stands in a sheltered hollow at the end of a narrow lane. It dates from 1724 but older tombstones and the fragment of an Anglian cross shaft formerly built into a wall of the church testify to earlier occupation. The map also marks the site of Morham Castle, of which there is no more trace than the adjacent village. Morham appears to have declined gradually rather than being deserted suddenly due to some catastrophe. There were still a few cottages here in the 1790s but the small size of the church suggests that even in the early eighteenth century the settlement was not large. The hamlet of Nenthorn near Kelso, provides an example of a shrunken village. Aerial photographs have revealed the foundations of buildings with associated trackways and field systems extending over a considerable area east of the present settlement and dating, presumably, from medieval or post-medieval times.

Other villages were re-sited or removed when landowners

Plate 7 The thatched seventeenth-century cottages at Swanston preserve the layout and character of the pre-improvement *ferm toun*

Plate 8 Remains of deserted farmsteads can often be seen among the Border hills. This example, at Whitropefoot in Liddesdale, dates from the nineteenth century

extended the parks around their mansions. The settlement of Bothans beside Yester House was removed for this reason at the end of the seventeenth century and replaced by the village of Gifford. A similar process occurred at Tyninghame in the later eighteenth century. Some settlements vanished when parishes were amalgamated and churches went out of use, though this could be a chicken-and-egg situation for parishes were sometimes amalgamated because one *kirk toun* had already declined. The parish of Bara in East Lothian was merged with Garvald in 1702 and all that remains are traces of the burial ground (642753); church and village alike have vanished.

Deserted *ferm touns* also exist too and may be more common than has sometimes been supposed. They tend to survive in marginal areas, on the fringes of later improved land. The flimsy nature of medieval and post-medieval Scottish houses means that individual structures leave little trace in the landscape. Because of constant rebuilding the sites of houses within a settlement tended to migrate so that one does not find the well-developed tofts and building platforms that characterise many English deserted village sites. Few deserted settlements have been excavated and securely dated. One example is Lour near Peebles (179358). Here you can see the foundations of a small tower house surrounded by a cluster of farm buildings within an enclosure which is the re-used ramparts of a small Iron Age fort. Around the settlement are traces of at least three types of ridge and furrow ploughing from different periods. The broader, more curving ridges may have been contemporary with the settlement. The excavators were fortunate to find artefacts such as clay pipes which showed that Lour had been inhabited into the seventeenth and eighteenth centuries.

A number of deserted settlements are clustered around the foundations of small tower houses. Lour has already been mentioned; Plora (359360) and Glentress (348432) near Innerleithen are other examples. Because buildings whose foundations are visible may not necessarily have been contemporary, and because many structures may have left no visible trace, it is difficult to decide whether these clusters were merely the outbuildings of the tower, the home farms of small estates, or larger settlements. Other remains are clearly those of single farmsteads with their outbuildings. An example can be seen beside the Stanhope Burn (146280). Here there is a building 30m (100ft) long with traces of three internal divisions, and another rectangular building close by. The main building was probably a house, barn and byre unit and there are traces of similar, less well preserved foundations nearby perhaps relating to an earlier farmstead. The continuity of occupation at this remote valley-head site is interesting. To the east of the farm are clearance cairns, banks and lynchets forming part of a Romano-British field system (Chapter 2). Above the farmstead are four platforms from an unenclosed settlement probably of Bronze Age date.

In some high-lying areas from which cultivation has retreated, like Coldingham Moor or the bleak plateau which fringes the western side of the Pentland Hills, it is possible to move from examining individual deserted sites to larger portions of the pre-improvement landscape. In these areas numbers of deserted farms have been identified, usually consisting of a rectangular building divided into two; probably a house and byre, with attached yards and a few acres of ridge and furrow ploughing.

SHIELINGS AND FORESTS

In early medieval times a system of transhumance was practised in which lowland livestock, with part of the community, were sent to summer pastures in the hills. There the people stayed, making butter and cheese and living in temporary huts. These summer settlements are known as shielings and their use continued in areas like the Outer Hebrides into living memory.

In the hills of southern Scotland the former occurrence of transhumance is shown by place names incorporating the medieval English elements 'shield', 'shiels' or 'shiel', denoting a shieling. However, the fact that such places are generally farms demonstrates how the frontiers of colonisation advanced by the conversion of temporary shielings to permanent settlements. Although there are only indirect hints in the fragmentary documentary record of medieval times, it is likely that in this area, as throughout Western Europe, there was a build up of population between the eleventh and early fourteenth century, with a corresponding expansion of settlement. This was aided by a period of warm climate which allowed cultivation to reach altitudes which have never been attained since. In the Lammermuirs, and probably other upland areas too, the expansion of commercial sheep farming by the Border abbeys in the twelfth and thirteenth centuries brought the use of summer shielings to an end and large monastic farms or granges were established at former shieling sites.

The shieling tradition survived longest in areas which were reserved during medieval times as hunting forests for the Crown or major landowners. Earlier hunting preserves may have existed but the system was extended under David I, a keen hunter, another of the institutions of Anglo-Norman England which he introduced to Scotland. In the twelfth and thirteenth centuries large parts of the Pentlands and Moorfoots, Eskdale and Liddesdale, the country between the Gala and Leader Waters, and many other smaller areas, were reserved for hunting. The largest hunting preserve of all was Ettrick Forest which comprised most of the valleys of the Ettrick and Yarrow Waters. In these forests settlement, agriculture, indeed any activities which might interfere with the supply of game, were strictly controlled. From the thirteenth century, however, there was growing pressure, particularly from the church, to release this under-utilised land for more progressive development. Abbeys like Melrose obtained rights of pasture in Ettrick Forest and the Lammermuirs, but they expressly forbade the monks to establish permanent settlements and must have involved the use of temporary shielings. Some hunting reserves survived into the fourteenth and fifteenth centuries, but many areas were gradually disafforested and opened up for colonisation. Livestock farms or 'forest stedes' were established in former forest areas like Eskdale, Liddesdale and particularly Ettrick Forest.

In later times game was restricted to specially constructed deer parks surrounded either by stone walls or earthworks and paling fences. A number of these are shown on sixteenth-century maps but few are visible in the modern landscape. One example is at Hermitage in Liddesdale on the hillside north of the medieval castle. A stone dyke, still some 2m (6.5ft) high in places, crudely built compared with later walls, marks the boundary of the deer park associated with the castle.

Ettrick Forest, which came back into Crown hands in 1455, was only opened up for settlement in the late fifteenth and sixteenth centuries. The forest *stedes*, inhabited by rangers and wardens, were turned into large commercial sheep farms, some held by the Crown, others leased to tenants. If you examine the modern map you will see that some of these farms, sited in the main valleys, are paired with others which have the same name plus the element 'shiel' and are situated in more remote, high-lying locations. For example the farms of Easter and Wester Deloraine beside the Ettrick Water have Deloraineshiel, nearly 5km (3 miles) away at an altitude of over 300m (980ft). This must originally have been a shieling for the forest *stede* but was permanently colonised at a later date, probably during the sixteenth century. The relatively late survival of transhumance in Ettrick Forest is shown by the remains of groups of shieling huts like those above Blackhouse on the Douglas Burn (275278) and in the neighbouring valley of the Mountbenger Burn (306263).

FIELD AND PASTURE

If many elements of the pre-improvement settlement pattern have survived, what of the fields and pastures which surrounded them? In looking for the remains of former cultivation we must distinguish between how farming was organised, how the land was divided between the cultivators, and how the land was cultivated. The first element may survive in the form of old field boundaries, but only the last is likely to leave much of an imprint in the landscape. Pre-improvement systems of cultivation have left little trace due to the extent of changes in the eighteenth and nineteenth centuries. Earlier field patterns are only recoverable in fragments from early estate plans and on the ground from around deserted settlements.

Fig 8 The Lothians and the Borders: land quality

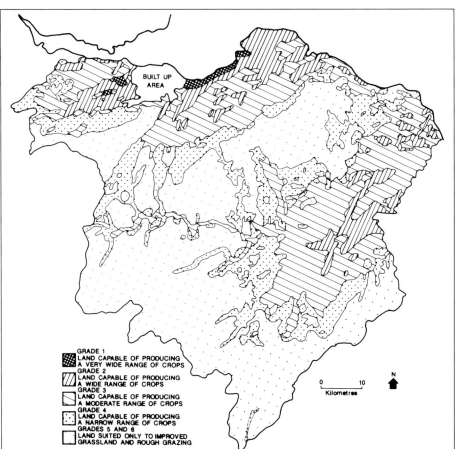

The arable lands of most townships were cultivated by a system known as infield-outfield. This was a variant of the open-field farming found throughout Britain in medieval and later times. The arable land had no permanent internal boundaries, the strips and blocks belonging to different cultivators being unenclosed and intermingled. The infield, usually the most fertile ground adjacent to the settlement, was cultivated intensively with a continuous rotation of cereals, generally bere (a hardy form of barley) and oats, with wheat and legumes on the best soils. The infield received most of the manure from the livestock but even so the scourging rotations that were used reduced crop yields.

The outfield was cultivated solely with oats and manured mainly by the temporary folding of livestock on the land during the summer. Plots of outfield were ploughed and sown with oats for a few years until yields fell to an unacceptable level. The land was then left to revert to rough pasture for a few years until it was ready to be cultivated once more. Around a third of the outfield was cropped in any one year. Lands within each township were divided between the occupiers by a system known as 'runrig'. The cultivators held their lands as shares which were allocated on the basis of both the quality and quantity of the land. This inevitably involved fragmentation into large numbers of strips and parcels as everyone received a portion of the best and the worst land. In early times the shares may have been re-allocated regularly but by the sixteenth and seventeenth centuries they had mostly become fixed.

The arable land was ploughed in parallel ridges and hollows running roughly downslope, the ridges often being about 4.5–5.5m (15–18ft) wide. This 'ridge and furrow' was created by the clumsy ploughs drawn by teams of eight or more oxen which were used well into the eighteenth century. The practice of ploughing a strip of land from the centre outwards threw the furrow slice constantly towards the middle producing, through time, a ridge while the boundaries of the strips, from which soil was constantly being removed, became the furrows. Ploughing ridge and furrow helped to demarcate shares in an open field system: a plot could be defined as a single ridge or a block of them. It was also a primitive but effective form of drainage in the days before underground tile drains became general. Water drained from the crests of the ridges to the furrows and then downslope into open field drains. The disadvantage of this system was that in a dry year the grain on the crests of the ridges might be parched while in a wet summer the crops in the bottom of the furrows might be waterlogged; but it ensured that some of the corn would thrive no matter what the weather!

Ridge and furrow continued in use into the early nineteenth century. Pre-improvement ridge and furrow can be recognised by the ridges being wider, more irregular, and curving in a reverse S-shape which may have resulted from ploughmen trying to ease their cumbersome teams round before reaching the ends of the strips. However, much of the ridge and furrow which you can see above modern cultivation, or preserved on golf courses, dates from the Napoleonic Wars when grain prices were high and much marginal land was ploughed up. Ridge and furrow from the period of improvement in the later eighteenth and early nineteenth century is generally narrower and more regular than that from earlier times.

Vestiges of old field systems can be seen at some sites where later cultivation has not obliterated them. The three superimposed systems of cultivation ridges at Lour have already been mentioned. The earliest ones, broad, high and curving, were probably associated with the deserted settlement which was occupied into the seventeenth and early eighteenth centuries. Even more complex is a site at Old Thornilee (4136) near Innerleithen. Here the foundations of three buildings lie alongside a disused track. Their appearance suggests a farmstead with two cottages and attached kaleyards, small enclosures in which kale and other vegetables were grown. Above and below them on the hillside can be traced a series of field systems covering some 12ha (30 acres). The earliest features, which may once have been more extensive, are horizontal terraces. These may have been far older than the settlement. Most of them have been obliterated by a series of oblique lynchets, breaks of slope caused by the gradual accumulation of soil on the upper side of a field boundary and its removal on the downslope side. The boundaries appear to have been stone walls defining a series of long strip fields, an arrangement which has no known parallels in this area. The lynchets have in turn been modified and partly obliterated by more conventional cultivation ridges running down the slope. The relative chronology of these cultivation systems is clear but not their absolute date although it has been presumed that the strip fields and overlying ridges are medieval or later.

Another type of field system can be seen in many places in the upper Tweed valley and its tributaries. These are cultivation terraces, usually running across steepish hillsides. They often occur in groups; one of the best examples is near Romannobridge on a steep slope above the Lyne Water (163470). Little is known about their date and origin. They are rare elsewhere in Scotland though similar terraces are widespread in England from the Pennines to the chalk downlands of the south. That they were produced by cultivation is shown at one or two sites where they gradually change into ridge and furrow on more gently sloping ground. In such cases they may have been formed by ploughing in strips across, rather than down, a slope. Under such circumstances the soil would tend to be removed from the upper part of the strip and accumulate at the downslope edge, gradually forming a terrace feature. This makes their formation sound almost accidental but on steeper ground, as at Roman-nobridge the terraces must have been deliberately constructed with pick and spade to create level surfaces for cultivation.

The date of these features is a puzzle. The association with ridge and furrow suggests that some examples are linked with open-field cultivation. This would place them at some time between the medieval period and the eighteenth century. However, there is no reason to suppose that because the various groups of terraces resemble each other they were necessarily all created and used at the same time. Some writers have suggested an Anglo-Saxon date for them. At Glenrath such terraces are certainly later than the small square plots of the Romano-British village. Their concentration in the hilly areas of south-east Scotland fits in with the maximum likely extent of Anglian occupation, though their distribution is wider than that of surviving Anglian place names. This could be mere coincidence though. At Bucht Knowe (840201) and Hayhope Knowe (806176) cultivation terraces seem to predate scooped enclosure sites of probable Romano-British date. It is possible that many groups of terraces have been destroyed and that they have only survived in the upper Tweed valley because cultivation and settlement have been less intensive here. If so, then the present-day distribution of such features may not reflect their former occurrence. On balance the terraces were probably created during a wide range of periods from prehistoric to medieval times.

In hill areas like the Lammermuirs where slopes are gentle, traces of ridge and furrow can be found at high altitudes – in places at up to 400m (1300ft). Close examination will sometimes show traces of associated settlements. This high-level cultivation probably dates from the medieval warm phase when average temperatures were higher than today, allowing crops to ripen at altitudes which would now be impossible. Medieval farmers may have cultivated well-drained slopes like these in preference to flatter more poorly-drained ground at lower altitudes.

The desertion of high-lying fields and steadings can be detected in the documentary record during subsequent centuries as the climate worsened, reaching its nadir at the end of the seventeenth century. However, the mid-eighteenth century Military Survey shows that

Plate 9 Curving pre-improvement ridge and furrow on a slope in the Lammermuir Hills

cultivation levels were still higher than would be considered worthwhile today. These upland farms were mainly pastoral ones whose tenants grew some grain for their own consumption. As they were not trying to grow cereals commercially like modern farmers they could put up with a much lower return. As we shall see in Chapter 6, a process of rationalisation began in the second half of the eighteenth century whereby large areas of high, exposed land were abandoned and much uncultivated ground at lower levels brought under the plough.

A major problem of pre-improvement farming was the limited amount of animal fodder produced from the arable land. No sown grasses or root crops were grown and much of the straw from the cereal crops was needed for thatching and other purposes. Natural hay was harvested from boggy lands beside streams and in hollows which were too wet to cultivate. Animals were grazed on the stubble after harvest, on those areas of outfield which were in fallow and on areas of rough pasture but often there was not enough grazing. In some districts, however, additional pasture was available as commonties, areas whose ownership was shared between two or more landowners and which were used by all their tenants. Commonties were a multi-purpose resource, for as well as grazing they provided peat for fuel, turf for roofing, stone for building and many other necessities.

Shortage of pasture elsewhere kept commonties in existence. People with rights to the use of a commonty guarded them jealously and resisted encroachments on the pasture. Many townships on better soils in the Merse had expanded their arable lands so that by the seventeeth or early eighteenth centuries the only grazing they had left was the area of outfield which was left unploughed from year to year. The only way that farmers in such areas could keep their livestock in reasonable shape was to send them away to commonties during the summer. Coldingham Moor, covering over 2,400ha (6,000 acres), was one of the largest and animals were sent to it from miles around. As will be described in more detail in Chapter 6 most commonties were divided up in the eighteenth and nineteenth centuries to provide land for cultivation or improved pasture but place names incorporating the word 'common' often indicate their former existence.

MARKETS AND FAIRS

In medieval times, and indeed much later, the villages of the Lothians and the Merse were primarily agricultural settlements. However, they were also places where business was transacted and goods exchanged. They probably functioned as market centres from early times but during the sixteenth and seventeenth centuries, with the development of a more commercial economy and slowly increasing prosperity, there was a growth of trading throughout the country-side. This was emphasised by the granting of market rights to many villages. The earliest grants carried the title 'burgh of barony' and the landowners who obtained burgh charters had, in theory, the right to plan fully-fledged towns and to endow them with burgesses, a council and a burgh court. The burghs which grew into towns were mainly coal- and salt-producing centres like Bo'ness, Prestonpans and Tranent, or older baronial foundations like Dalkeith and Musselburgh.

Where villages were purely agricultural it is doubtful if there was ever any serious intention by their proprietors to develop them into towns. Most of them merely provided markets and fairs which served the farms within their parish. During the later seventeenth century this was increasingly recognised by the granting of market rights to villages like East Linton, Ormiston and Stenton without the pretentious title of 'burgh'.

Whether designated as a burgh of barony or merely a licensed

Plate 10 The mercat cross at Ancrum dominates the small triangular green of this former baronial burgh

market centre, the symbol of a village's right to carry on trade was its mercat cross. The finest surviving one is at Preston, East Lothian (389739). It stands on a stone drum nearly 4m (13ft) high with a platform on top from which proclamations could be read. The shaft which rises from this rotunda is topped by a unicorn holding a tablet bearing the design of a lion rampant. Many 'crosses', like the one at Preston, are not actually topped by a cross; some have a stone ball as at Gifford or even a sundial like the one at Pencaitland. Ormiston has a genuine cross of pre-Reformation origin which predates the granting of market rights to the village. It was probably transferred from a chapel which once stood nearby.

DOVECOTS AND MILLS

Although the rural landscape was transformed in the eighteenth and nineteenth centuries one feature typifying the old order has survived in considerable numbers: dovecots (or 'doocots' as they are known north of the Border). Dovecots were a perquisite of landed proprietors and this explains why so many are adjacent to castles or mansions. They are more common in the Lothians and the Merse than in the Tweed valley because estates in these areas were smaller and more numerous, and supplies of grain, on which the pigeons fed, more plentiful. Pigeons were a valuable source of fresh meat in winter. Their manure was also highly prized as a fertiliser. However, pigeons made great depredations on surrounding crops. A statute of 1617 restricted the construction of dovecots to proprietors who had a rent income of 10 chalders of grain from lands within 3km (2 miles) of the proposed site. The aim was to ensure that the birds fed mainly at the expense of the landowner's tenants rather than those of his neighbours.

Dovecots were stone structures with hundreds of ledges inside for the birds to nest on and holes for them to fly in and out. The oldest surviving examples date from the sixteenth century. One at Athelstaneford (533734) is dated 1583 and another at Tranent (403734) 1587. Early dovecots are of two main types. The first is beehive-shaped, circular in section and tapering towards the top like a fat pepperpot. They usually have protruding string-courses running round the outside to prevent rats from climbing in and destroying the eggs. Good examples can be seen at Dirleton Castle, near Preston Mill (515839) where the interior of the dovecot can be inspected, and two in the village of Preston (389739). The other early style, typified by the one at Athelstaneford, is a rectangular 'lectern' type, so-called because of its sloping top. Dovecots usually face south to

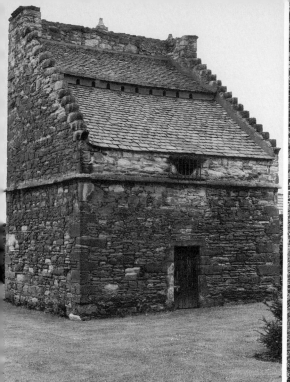

Plate 11 A lectern-type dovecot near Preston Tower, with a set of flight holes and suitable perches on the south-facing crow-step gables

Plate 12 The grain mill at Kirkton Manor, with its overgrown lade, is an example of the type of larger estate mill which was built in the late eighteenth and early nineteenth centuries

give the birds a sunny surface to sit on while sheltering them from northerly winds. They continued to be built into the eighteenth century and late examples have a variety of styles from Scottish baronial to classical. Smaller dovecots could accommodate around 500 birds while the larger ones housed up to 2,000.

Another widespread feature of the pre-Improvement countryside was the corn mill. Small water-powered grain mills were found in almost every village and many hamlets. An upland valley like Manor Water near Peebles, with only a scattering of farms, had four of them. There was generally at least one per estate because milling was, like possessing a dovecot, a landowners' monopoly. Proprietors' feudal rights included thirlage, the right to compel their tenants to grind their grain at the estate mill. The landowner provided the capital for constructing the mill which was then leased to a miller for a substantial rent. The miller recouped his rent and made a profit by charging the tenants multures, a fixed proportion of the grain which they brought to be ground, often about a sixteenth. In addition tenants frequently had to help repair the mill and bring home new millstones. Although it was widely resented by farmers, thirlage was so profitable for landowners that it was not abolished in many areas until the early nineteenth century.

Because mills had a monopoly over a limited area they were generally small, primitive and not very efficient. Most have disappeared leaving only a few streamside foundations or a place name. A fine example has, however, been preserved at Preston Mill near East Linton (595779). The National Trust for Scotland have restored it to working order; you can have a guided tour of the machinery and learn about the intricacies of milling. The fabric of the mill probably dates from the eighteenth century but the adjoining corn-drying kilns, essential in an uncertain climate where the harvest was often gathered late and wet, may be older. The picturesque appearance of the mill with its sandstone walls, and red pantiled roofs emphasises how well such small-scale industries blended in with rural life before the Agricultural Revolution. The River Tyne, which provided power for the mill, was often a fickle friend, as the flood marks on the walls of the mill show.

There are more examples of a later generation of country mills which were larger, better built and more efficient but still water driven and built largely to serve local needs. Sandy's Mill on the Tyne above East Linton (551754) and West Saltoun Mill (469667) are examples from East Lothian while in Tweeddale ones at Blyth Bridge (131448) and Kirkton Manor (221379) have preserved their wheels.

HOUSE AND HOME

We know little about the homes of most of the inhabitants of this region in medieval and early-modern times. Virtually no ordinary domestic buildings predating the improved cottages of the eighteenth century have survived. There is a huge gap in the landscape record which is only bridged by low turf-covered foundations on a few deserted sites. The reason no structures have survived is that they were too flimsily built; most would not have lasted for more than a few years without major repairs or rebuilding. As a result they were easily cleared away when housing standards began to improve in the eighteenth century leaving only the occasional indeterminate foundations.

At Springwood Park near Kelso recent excavations have uncovered three primitive stone-walled, cruck-timbered houses with cobbled areas at one end which appear to have been occupied by livestock. The buildings dated from the late twelfth or thirteenth centuries.

Plate 13 Few thatched buildings survive in the Borders. This example, in the village of Denholm, was the birthplace of Dr John Leyden, a noted nineteenth-century antiquarian

Descriptions and estate records confirm that as late as the seventeenth century the normal home for a farming family in the seventeenth century was little different, with livestock and people still under a single roof.

Tenants and cottars were expected to build their own homes with whatever materials were available locally. Stones turned up from the soil by ploughing served for foundations and, cemented with clay or interlaid with turf, for the lower parts of the walls. Where clay was plentiful it sometimes formed the main walling material. The upper parts of the walls were often of turf construction. The roof was covered with turf and straw or heather thatch. The weight of the roof was carried by sets of cruck timbers against which the flimsy walls leaned. In a largely treeless countryside timber was in short supply and landowners were often niggardly in providing new roof beams, often expecting their tenants to shore up existing rotten timbers with odd pieces of wood. Under such circumstances it is not surprising that houses and outbuildings sometimes collapsed!

By the eighteenth century tenant farmers were more prosperous and housing conditions had improved. George Robertson described the houses of the better-off Lothian farmers in the 1760s on the eve of the most rapid phase of improvement. They were low-built and lit by only a few small windows, roofed with straw and turf, and had the farm dunghill right outside the front door. Inside they were divided into two main rooms, the but and the ben. The but was a kitchen and servants' apartment where the entire household met at mealtimes. The ben was the farmer's private quarters where he and his family slept at night and entertained friends. A low attic provided storage and sleeping accommodation for male farm servants. There was, at least, a proper fireplace and chimney stack in the gable to replace the open hearth in the centre of the floor and the smoke hole in the thatch which had been normal for farmers in earlier centuries and was still common for their cottars who lived in one-roomed hovels made of field stones and turf. The normal labourers' houses in Tweeddale at this time were sparsely furnished single-room buildings. If the labourer was fortunate enough to afford a cow, the animal shared this single room with the family, occupying a narrow area at one end partitioned off behind the box-beds.

Plate 14 Attractive farm workers' cottages at Drem, East Lothian. With solid stone walls and pantiled roofs these were a vast improvement on farm workers' accommodation a generation or two before

4
KIRK AND CROSS

CHRISTIANITY has influenced the lives of the inhabitants of the Lothians and the Borders for some 1,500 years. In this more secular age it is easy to forget how central was the role of the Church to everyday life in the past. During this long period the Church has influenced the landscape in many ways. The Christian legacy is most obvious in surviving buildings ranging from homely parish kirks, reflecting the simple beliefs and lifestyles of the ordinary rural population, through solid burgh churches which commemorate the wealth as well as the piety of late-medieval burgesses, to magnificent abbeys. It can be fascinating to hunt for the turf-covered foundations of a forgotten chapel high in a Border valley or to discover traces of Anglo-Norman sculpture built into a Georgian parish church. Religion has also influenced the landscape through patterns of parish organisation and landholding. The variety of this landscape heritage reflects the many-faceted role of a Church which was also a major landowner and political force. This chapter will trace some of the changing ways in which Christianity has found expression in the landscape through the centuries.

THE EARLY CHRISTIAN CHURCH

Early Christianity has left an indefinite imprint on the landscape. In the post-Roman period it has been argued that Christianity continued to survive at Carlisle and even that a series of dioceses based on early monastic sites such as Abercorn and Old Melrose was established in southern Scotland. Virtually nothing survives in the landscape apart from a few inscribed stones. The most notable, the Yarrow Stone, stands about a kilometre upstream from Yarrow church. It appears to have been associated with a number of burials, perhaps in a tribal cemetery. The stone commemorates two princes, Nudua and Dumnogenus, sons of Liberalis, who was presumably a local leader.

The Cat Stone, near Kirkliston, is similar. It is located on a circular

Fig 9 Some ecclesiastical sites in south-east Scotland

boundary enclosing a cemetery with burials laid out east-west in classic early-Christian style. Its inscription is harder to decipher than the one on the Yarrow Stone. 'In this tomb lies Vetta, daughter of Victricius' is one rendering. Other inscribed stones have been discovered at Kirkhope, south of Peebles, and Borthwick but have been removed to museums for safe keeping.

The Anglians seem to have taken over and developed the church. They established a monastery at Abercorn on the shores of the Forth in the late seventh century. There are no remains of the early church and its associated buildings there but part of the *vallum* or boundary wall of the monastery can be traced running through the later churchyard. Inside the attractive Norman church at Abercorn are preserved a fine Anglian cross shaft and a couple of hogback tombstones. At Coldingham a monastery was founded near St Abb's Head with houses for both monks and nuns. Two sets of foundations probably of churches, on sites a kilometre apart, one on a promontory cut off by a bank and ditch, the other on a hill

71

surrounded by an earthen rampart, may mark their locations.

Another early monastic site at Old Melrose is located within the neck of a meander of the Tweed a short way downstream from the great medieval abbey. There may have been a church here in the sixth century, established by missionaries from Carlisle. St Aidan, a monk from Iona, founded a Celtic monastery here in the mid-seventh century and it was at Old Melrose that St Cuthbert, one of the most influential religious figures of his day, lived as a novice before moving to Lindisfarne. The monastery at Old Melrose was destroyed in 859 by Kenneth, King of Scots, but some sort of religious life continued into early medieval times. No remains of any buildings associated with the monastery can be seen but cutting across the neck of the meander is an earthwork which may mark the boundary of the monastic precinct.

Apart from these earthworks and foundations the main evidence for Christianity during the Anglian period is a scattering of sculptured stones. The ones at Abercorn have already been mentioned. In the museum at Jedburgh Abbey is a fine panel dating from the seventh century. It is thought to have been part of the tomb of St Boisel, a contemporary of Cuthbert, which may originally have come from Old Melrose where Boisel was abbot. The museum also houses a fine tenth-century cross shaft.

Other fragments of Anglian sculpture have been discovered among the foundations of later parish churches during rebuilding. Part of a cross-shaft was formerly built into the wall of the parish church at Morham in East Lothian. The replica of another cross shaft can be seen in the church at Aberlady; both pieces have been transferred to the Royal Museum in Edinburgh. When the old parish church at Innerleithen was rebuilt in 1871 the base of an Anglian cross shaft was discovered among the foundations. It now stands outside the modern church. Another Anglian introduction to the area, derived from Norse influences, was the hogback tombstone. Designed as houses of the dead, hogbacks are carved to represent contemporary dwellings with shingles and curved roof ridges. They date from between the tenth and twelfth centuries. Two fine examples can be seen in the church at Abercorn and others are preserved in or adjacent to the churches at Ancrum, Bedrule, Edrom, Lempitlaw, Nisbet and Old Cambus in the Merse, and Stobo in Tweeddale.

EARLY PARISH KIRKS

One of many innovations introduced by the House of Canmore in the late eleventh and twelfth centuries, particularly in the reign of

David I (1124–53), was Norman architecture and the tradition of church building in stone on a large scale. There must already have been many churches in this area by the mid-eleventh century, linked to monasteries or built by landowners. There is little sign of them in the landscape. Most were probably simple structures of timber or rough stonework like one which has recently been excavated at the Hirsel near Coldstream. It was a small, square building of rough cobbles and probably roofed with turf. It is thought to date from the tenth century and was easily obliterated by later building on the same site. Place names like Eccles in Berwickshire, Eaglescairnie near Haddington and Ecclesmachan in West Lothian hint at the sites of other early churches.

Fragments of Norman architecture survive in parish kirks throughout the area. This suggests that during the twelfth century there was an organised and sustained attempt to create a network of parishes and churches, built in stone and embodying the new architectural influences. The plans of these buildings were simple with rectangular naves and chancels and sometimes a square or apsidal sanctuary at the eastern end. Few have survived in anything like their original form. Norman features tend to occur as fragments built into later churches, or as abandoned ruins which have been robbed of most of their stonework. This is due to the way in which churches in this region developed. Where a church was in continuous use it was generally rebuilt as the population grew and architectural fashions changed. A high proportion of early churches were substantially altered or completely rebuilt in the eighteenth century and often again during the Victorian era. Sometimes the new church was built alongside the remains of the old one, as at Gladsmuir (458733) and North Berwick (554853). More frequently the new building was erected on the foundations of the old. At Pencaitland (444690) this has produced a comparatively modern kirk with a suspiciously early plan; the ghost of the medieval church survives in the layout of its successor.

In some cases, as at Gullane and Tyninghame, the site of the parish church was changed and the medieval building, though escaping later renovation, has fallen into ruin. At Tyninghame, near the site of the Dark Age monastery, are the remains of a twelfth-century church whose decoration is similar to or perhaps even finer than the one at Dalmeny, described below. Unfortunately only fragments survive. The church was in good condition in the seventeenth century but in 1761 the parishes of Tyninghame and Whitekirk were merged. The former church went out of use and was systematically dismantled. Another ruined early medieval church stands in the middle of the

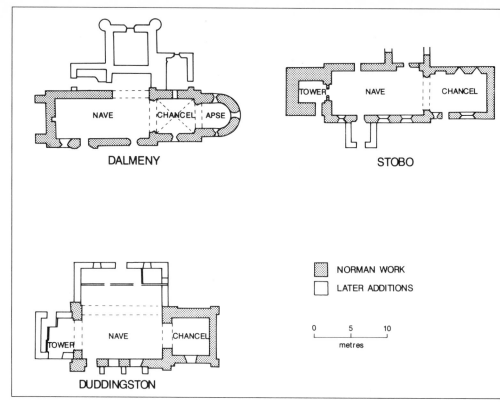

Fig 10 Plans of some typical Norman churches

modern golfing resort of Gullane (481827). Norman chevron design is still visible on the blocked up chancel arch. The church was abandoned in 1612 and worship transferred to nearby Dirleton because the settlement at Gullane was declining due to encroachment by windblown sand.

A number of Berwickshire churches preserve traces of Anglo-Norman masonry. At Bunkle (809597) the apse of an early church survives, the simplicity of the design suggesting that it dates from the late eleventh or early twelfth centuries. The remainder of the church was demolished in the early nineteenth century and the stones used to build a new church. Edrom (827558) has a fine Norman doorway with elaborate decoration. It survived because it was made into a burial vault. Legerwood church (594434) near Earlston preserves an attractive Norman chancel arch with the ruins of the original chancel. At Chirnside another fragment of Norman work survives in the south doorway.

Stobo church near Peebles was once the focus of a huge medieval parish covering most of the headwaters of the Tweed. Though altered and extended in later times, it is still essentially a Norman

74

church though, sadly, the original chancel arch was destroyed by Victorian 'restorers'. The gabled tower at the west end may also be early in date. One of the most attractive early churches is at Duddingston, now a suburb of Edinburgh. It stands on a rocky hillock overlooking a reed-fringed loch dominated by the bulk of Arthur's Seat. Although altered and extended in subsequent centuries it is still, essentially, a Norman church with the original arches over the south doorway and chancel surviving.

West Lothian also has several churches with traces of Norman work. Uphall parish church still has a twelfth-century tower, gable roofed like Stobo, and a Norman nave and chancel. At Abercorn a round-headed doorway with a distinctively sculptured panel remains from the Norman church which was built on the site of the seventh-century monastery. The parish church at Dalmeny (144775) is the most complete Norman church in Scotland, with a wealth of decoration, particularly around the south entrance and on the internal arches. It has a round apse at the eastern end and although additions have been made to the north side and a modern tower added at the west end, the south front and the east end are unchanged. The south entrance is richly decorated with an arcade of intersecting arches above and a line of Norman windows from nave

Plate 15 The parish church at Prestonkirk, East Lothian, mostly rebuilt in 1770, has a fine thirteenth-century chancel

Plate 16 Attractively set beside the River Tyne, the church of St Mary's, the burgh kirk of Haddington, is almost a cathedral in scale

to apse. Inside, the original Norman vaulting survives as well as the arches between.

Later medieval parish kirks in this area are disappointing. Few were extended or rebuilt due to turbulent political conditions and also because the revenues of many churches were appropriated by monastic houses which spent little on their upkeep. The parish church of Prestonkirk near East Linton (592799) is mostly a plain Georgian rebuilding dating from 1770 but a magnificent thirteenth-century chancel survives. Contemporary churches, more or less complete, survive at Bathgate in West Lothian, and Cockpen and Keith to the east of Edinburgh. Unlike twelfth-century churches there was no chancel arch and no difference in width between nave and chancel. These later kirks were simple rectangular boxes, a style which remained characteristic of Scottish churches throughout the Middle Ages. The fourteenth century produced few churches due to frequent warfare with England and internal unrest. The ruined one at Temple with its attractive architectural details is one of the best examples.

Although Scottish rural churches are generally modest and homely, some in the older burghs are more impressive reflecting the greater wealth of urban communities in the fourteenth and fifteenth centuries. Civic pride was sometimes expressed by financing large and richly-ornamented burgh kirks. South-east Scotland has three outstanding examples. St Giles in Edinburgh will be described in Chapter 9. The other two are St Mary's in Haddington and St Michael's in Linlithgow. Both have superb settings, the former away from the town centre beside the still waters of the River Tyne, the latter sharing a rocky promontory above Linlithgow Loch with the adjacent royal palace. St Mary's is not hemmed in by other buildings and this helps to emphasise its size. It is almost a cathedral in scale, slightly larger than St Giles in Edinburgh and, unlike it, built in a relatively short period and not greatly altered thereafter. It has a cruciform plan with aisles to the nave and choir. The imposing central tower was designed to carry a distinctive crown spire but it seems that one was never actually built. The plan of St Michael's is more like a large English parish church, with a western tower, an aisled nave and choir, and short transepts. It once had a crown spire but this was dismantled in 1821 to be replaced by a striking modern one in 1964.

MEDIEVAL ABBEYS

Celtic and Anglian monastic communities in south-east Scotland were in decline by the eleventh century partly due to Viking raids and other internal conflicts. Into this vacuum David I and his successors introduced monastic orders which had originated on the continent and had become established in England following the Norman Conquest. Monasteries were yet another Anglo-Norman innovation which helped to shape the medieval Scottish landscape. Although the Benedictines had been established at Coldingham in 1098 by King Edgar, David I favoured the new, stricter rule of the Cistercians. Together with the Augustinian canons the Cistercians dominated Scottish monasticism but other orders like the Premonstratensians who founded Dryburgh and the Tironensian monks who established themselves at Kelso also played a part. The heyday of monastic foundation was the twelfth and thirteenth centuries but many houses remained vigorous and active into the sixteenth century, as is shown in the fabric of abbeys like Melrose by large-scale rebuilding programmes. In addition, other orders appeared including various groups of friars who settled in the burghs. Some of their houses, like that of the Observantine friars in Jedburgh, which has recently been excavated, appear to have prospered until destroyed by the English invasions of the 1520s and 1540s.

Plate 17 The eastern end of Melrose Abbey, showing the exuberant and highly-decorated rebuilding of the fifteenth century

Plate 18 At Dryburgh Abbey the remains of the domestic buildings around the cloister are well preserved

Among the earliest and wealthiest monastic foundations in Scotland were the great Border abbeys of Melrose, Dryburgh, Kelso and Jedburgh. In the sixteenth century their organisation collapsed under the impact of the English invasions of the 1540s and the Reformation in 1560. Impressive in ruin even today, it is worth considering them individually. They serve as blueprints for reconstructing other monasteries like Coldingham or Newbattle whose remains are scanty, and the differences in their layout and architecture provide many insights into the lives of the monks who lived and worshipped in them.

In 1136 David I granted land at Melrose for the foundation of a new Cistercian house and a group of monks was sent from Rievaulx in Yorkshire to establish the community. Instead of settling at Old Melrose on the site of the early-Christian monastery they chose a location a short distance upstream. Perhaps the meander loop on which the original monastery had stood was too restricted. Recently it has been suggested that a pre-existing church, previously thought to have been at Old Melrose, might actually have stood on the site of the new monastery and that the Cistercians incorporated the nave of this into their first church. This would explain how the new church was dedicated only ten years after the monks arrived. A wall which might, on this interpretation, have been the west wall of the pre-Cistercian church, is still visible. The rebuilding of Melrose in the fifteenth century, beginning at the eastern end, lost momentum before it reached, and destroyed, this early stonework.

At Melrose, as with most medieval monasteries, the buildings surrounding the cloister in which the monks lived and worked have not survived as well as the abbey church. One reason for this, at Melrose and elsewhere, was that after the Reformation the church, albeit in a ruined state, was still used for worship by the parish community while the buildings around the cloister merely served as a convenient quarry. At Melrose the domestic buildings have been reduced to their foundations. Despite this, their layout is more clear and complete than at other Border abbeys. The organisation of the domestic buildings of a medieval monastery usually followed a standard pattern. The cloister was normally located to the south of the church to maximise the amount of sunlight and protect the area from northerly winds. At Melrose the cloister lies north of the church, probably to facilitate the provision of water. Strangely, it was the location of the latrine block, which needed a constant supply of water, that determined the position of the cloister and even the church. At Melrose the obvious source of water was the River Tweed which lay to the north and it was sensible to locate the domestic

buildings in this direction. The monks constructed a canal over 2km (1.2 miles) long which ran from the river providing drinking water, powering the abbey's corn mill and flushing out the latrines further downstream. This canal can still be seen beside the abbey and was modelled on a similar one at the mother house of Rievaulx.

As well as the monks who officiated in the abbey church Cistercian houses like Melrose also housed large numbers of lay brethren who did various manual tasks. The community probably included several hundred people at its maximum and the ranges of domestic buildings at Melrose are the largest in Scotland. Most of the abbey church dates from a period of rebuilding which began after the abbey was burnt by the English in 1385 and which continued, intermittently, into the sixteenth century. The parts of the church which date from

80

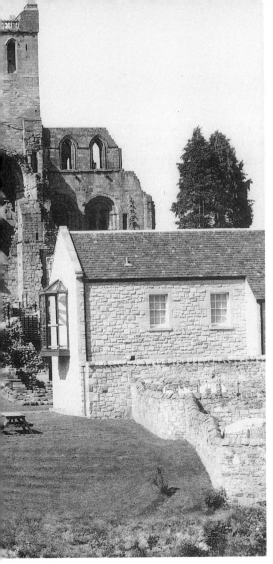

the twelfth century are plain, almost severe but the rebuilt eastern end is ornate, elaborate and exuberant. It has huge windows with delicate tracery and a wealth of carving, including such grotesque gargoyles as a pig playing a set of bagpipes! The master mason responsible for some of the best work came from northern England but French influences can also be detected: fifteenth-century Melrose was no backwater but was in the mainstream of European architectural development. The detached building to the north of the abbey may originally have been the abbot's house. It was remodelled around 1590 as a house for the lay commendator who took charge of the abbey and its land after the Reformation.

Dryburgh Abbey, 5km (3 miles) away on the opposite bank of the Tweed, is peacefully set among woods and parkland and has been

81

described as the loveliest medieval site in Scotland. It was founded in 1150 by Hugh de Morville, David I's Constable, one of the few Scottish monasteries founded by a noble. The site was granted to the Premonstratensian canons, a more ascetic offshoot of the Augustinians. Dryburgh was never as wealthy as Melrose because its initial land grant was smaller but it suffered a similar fate at the hands of English armies in the fourteenth century and again in the sixteenth. Here, however, it is the church that is badly ruined while the buildings around the cloister are better preserved. The cloister stands south of the church, on the classic pattern, and a deep artificial channel led water from the Tweed past the south range of domestic buildings.

About 1113 monks were brought to Scotland by David I from the reformed Benedictine house of Tiron in France and were settled in the neighbourhood of Selkirk. For some reason this location proved unsuitable and within a decade the monks had moved to a site beside the Tweed at Kelso close to the royal castle of Roxburgh. Here they founded a monastery which was second only to Melrose in wealth. The monastic buildings of the abbey have vanished and all that remains of the church is the late twelfth-century west end and the north transept with its magnificent gable. This is tragic for the ruins indicate that the church must have been one of the finest Romanesque buildings in Scotland with transepts at both ends in a style derived from Carolingian churches in the Rhineland. The church was burnt by English forces several times between the fourteenth and the mid-sixteenth centuries. After the Reformation a parish kirk and later a school were created within the ruined nave but most of the stonework was robbed. Nevertheless, even in its badly ruined state the church stands as one of the finest survivals of Norman architecture in Scotland.

Jedburgh, founded around 1138 as a house for Augustinian canons, has the best-preserved church of any of the Border abbeys, dominating the burgh which grew around it and attractively set overlooking the Jed Water. The cloister and monastic buildings, which were terraced into the steep slope between the church and the river, have been reduced to their foundations but the nave of the church is intact though roofless. The west front of the church is the finest twelfth-century façade in Scotland, similar in many respects to the more poorly-preserved remains at Kelso. Inside the nave the heavy piers supporting the Romanesque arcades give an impression of power and strength which is lightened by the more graceful clerestory above.

Early Christian monasteries had been simple, ascetic communities but David I and his successors made huge gifts of land to the new abbeys. The initial grant to Melrose was over 5,000 acres and this was extended by later donations. The property of Melrose included arable land in the Tweed valley but the real wealth of the Cistercians lay in the hills. The monks acquired grazing rights to over 6,900ha (17,000 acres) of upland waste between the Leader and Gala Waters as well as pastures in the Cheviots and Teviotdale. The Cistercians developed these areas as huge sheep ranges. Melrose built up a flock of around 12,500 sheep, the largest of any Border abbey, and wool was a major revenue earner for the monks. The monastic farms, called granges, were worked by groups of lay brothers. The name sometimes survives in modern place names, like Drygrange near the junction of the Tweed and Leader Water.

There are few traces today of these communal monastic farms but at Penshiel (641632), high in the Lammermuirs, the remains of one which formerly belonged to Melrose Abbey can be seen. The name suggests that this may originally have been a shieling, where livestock were grazed in summer. If so, it was replaced by a permanent sheep farm staffed by Cistercian lay brothers. The surviving walling is still 3m (10ft) high with signs of a vault above the ground floor rooms and an outside staircase. Fainter traces of other buildings surrounding a courtyard can also be seen.

The ruins of the great Border abbeys are still impressive but there were many other monastic foundations in south-east Scotland. Some, like Newbattle Abbey, a daughter house of Melrose, or the Cistercian nunnery east of Haddington, have disappeared almost entirely. At Coldingham the Benedictines built a large thirteenth-century church as the focus of their abbey. Only fragments of the transepts and the north and east walls of the choir survive. In 1662 these were incorporated into a new building which still serves as the parish church, but the arcaded interior is a splendid one.

Fragments of the churches of other establishments survived because they were converted into parish kirks after the Reformation or adapted as burial vaults. An interesting example is Soutra Aisle (452584), a low vaulted building roofed with flagstones which stands on an isolated ridge over 350m (1200ft) up on the bleak moors between the Lothians and Lauderdale. It stands close to Dere Street and the Girthgate, the set of medieval trackways which followed its line. Halfway between Edinburgh and the Border abbeys, it was founded in the mid-twelfth century as a hospice for pilgrims and travellers and was endowed with lands in the surrounding lowlands. After the Reformation it fell into ruin for it was too remote to be used as a parish church. Most of the fabric was removed to build enclosure walls and farmsteads during the nineteenth century but part of the church, appropriated as a burial vault for a local landowning family, was left intact. The small surviving building gives a poor impression of the size of the original hospice with its church, infirmary and pilgrims' accommodation.

Another interesting survival is Torphicen Preceptory in West Lothian. This was the Scottish headquarters of the Knights of St John. A church was built here in the twelfth century with a cruciform plan and a central tower. During the fifteenth century the transepts and tower were rebuilt to give a fortress-like appearance which echoes contemporary tower-house design. After the Reformation the nave was used as the local parish church until the mid-eighteenth century when a replacement was built alongside. The nave and choir of the church, together with the domestic buildings of the knights, have vanished. The transept and tower were preserved as a courthouse for the local landowner. In the adjacent churchyard stands a stone inscribed with a cross. This is believed to mark the centre of a circular sanctuary area which surrounded the Preceptory. A circuit of 'refuge stones', some of which still survive, lay about a kilometre and a half from the church marking the boundary of the area within which fugitives could seek protection.

COLLEGIATE CHURCHES

In the fifteenth century it became fashionable for landowners to found collegiate churches in which groups or 'colleges' of priests headed by a provost held services with more ceremony than was possible in an ordinary parish church, saying masses for the souls of the founders and their families. Some collegiate churches developed from private chapels, others from parish churches. These private churches were often lavishly endowed and south-east Scotland has some impressive examples. Several of them were never completed though. The finances of the families that endowed them were insufficient or the Reformation intervened to halt construction. In most cases the choir, and sometimes the transepts, were built but the nave was never added, as at Seton, Roslin and Crichton.

The collegiate church at Dunglass (768719) survived destruction during the English invasions of the 1540s but following the Reformation it was converted into a barn and stable. One gable was broken to allow access for carts and rows of holes in the vaulting show where timber floors were slotted in. Nevertheless it is still largely intact, an attractive church though more severe and plain than other collegiate foundations. It is cruciform in plan with a low

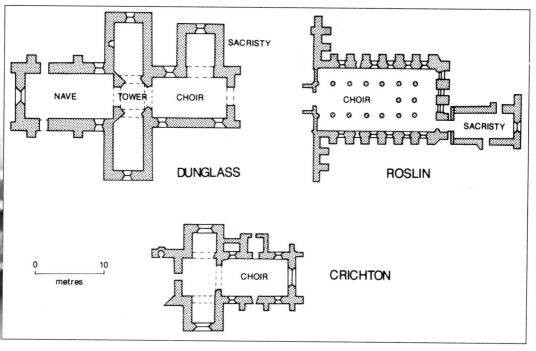

Fig 11 Some examples of collegiate churches

tower over the crossing. Its founder, Sir Alexander Hume of
Dunglass, received permission to establish a collegiate church here
in 1450 but there may have been an earlier private chapel on the site.

The church at Dunglass was built more or less at one period but
the one at Seton (419751), is more composite. The nave of the church
was either never completed or was demolished after the Reformation
when the church went out of use. What survives are the transepts,
choir and tower of a church whose plan was similar to Dunglass but
whose architecture was more ornate, with a fine polygonal apse. The
first phase of construction appears to date from the 1430s and
successive generations of Setons extended and embellished the
building: the transepts and tower were added as late as the 1540s.
Unlike Dunglass, which is rather dark inside, Seton is light and airy
and the large windows have preserved much of their tracery. The
foundations of the living quarters for the priests who officiated at
the church can be seen nearby.

The most glorious product of the Scottish collegiate movement is
Roslin Chapel. Standing near the castle of the Sinclairs, overlooking
the river North Esk, Roslin is remarkable not for its size, but for the
riot of Gothic carving which covers every part, interior and exterior,
an exuberance which contrasts with the severe, plain style of most
late-medieval Scottish architecture. The interior is particularly

Plate 20 The uncharacteristically rich decoration of Roslin Chapel makes it Scotland's finest collegiate church

impressive; the stone-vaulted roof is encrusted with sculpture to the point of eccentricity. Most fantastic of all is the celebrated 'Prentice Pillar', one of the internal columns, which is carved with designs which spiral round the column. Tradition has it that the pillar was carved by a talented apprentice, during his master's absence, and that the craftsman, on his return, killed the lad out of envy! A more prosaic explanation is that the name derives from a member of the Prentys family, skilled English sculptors who might have been called in to work on the chapel. The vocabulary of Scottish architectural historians tends to run out of control when they describe Roslin for the building is in a class of its own. Founded by William St Clair, Earl of Caithness and Orkney, on the site of an earlier chapel, it was under construction by 1446. Like Seton, the church lacks a nave; only the choir and parts of the east walls of the transepts were built.

AFTER THE REFORMATION

The Reformation in 1560 brought important changes to the ways in which churches were used. The abbeys, priories, nunneries and friaries were deliberately defaced, allowed to decay, and often systematically plundered of their stone. The form of worship changed and with it the layout of parish kirks. There was now no barrier between congregation and clergy so that the medieval division of churches into nave and chancel, with transepts and chapels, became redundant. Pulpits were re-sited in the centre of the south wall with pews facing them from all directions and churches became open rectangular boxes with unencumbered views from end to end. The reformed church did not allow burial inside their kirks. This explains the lack of post sixteenth-century burial monuments in Scottish churches and the number of family burial vaults or aisles attached to churches or standing nearby. A feature of many post-Reformation churches was a separate gallery of 'laird's loft' for the local landowning family, reflecting the fact that the patronage of parish churches was now in lay hands. At Abercorn the loft for the Earls of Hopetoun has an adjoining retiring room where the family could relax and take meals between services! At Bowden (554301) there is also a retiring room behind the laird's loft, with a private

Plate 21 Two monuments and an ancient cross base at Old Kirkhope, Manor Water, may mark the site of a forgotten medieval chapel. An early Christian inscribed stone was discovered nearby, indicating that this site had Christian connections from very early times

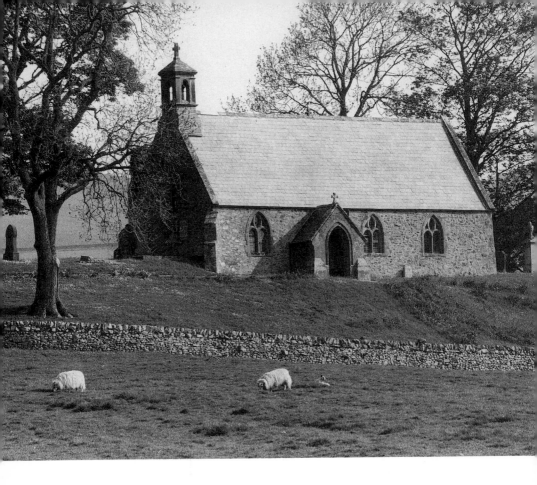

burial aisle below, a feature which occurs in other churches built after 1560.

One of the most attractive post-Reformation kirks is at Lyne, west of Peebles on a site which may originally have been occupied by a chapel of the medieval church of Stobo. Prominently set on a hillock and framed by mature trees it is a simple rectangle with a small belfry in place of a tower. It was built with funds provided by Lord Hay in the early 1640s. The original oak pulpit and Lord Hay's canopied pew still survive. Several post-Reformation churches adopted a T-plan, the wing housing the laird's loft and burial aisle being balanced by a tower on the opposite side of the building. The harled and whitewashed church at Gifford (535681) and the one at Carrington (319607), both dating from 1710, are good examples. The simple rectangular plan with a gable belfry at one end and a porch in the south wall of an otherwise plain exterior characterised most eighteenth- and nineteenth-century churches like the ones at Morebattle and Sprouston although more refined architecture is sometimes evident as in the classical-style church at Penicuik, dating from 1770.

The more secular role of kirk sessions, groups of lay elders who were responsible for maintaining religious and moral discipline in each parish, is sometimes visible. Several churches have fixed to their exterior walls sets of jougs, or iron neck bands, by which offenders could be secured. In later times the activities of 'Resurrectionists' or body snatchers who dug up corpses to sell to the Edinburgh medical schools, led to a careful watch being kept over churchyards. Watch houses can still be seen at Glencorse, Spott and Pencaitland.

The tombstones which surround parish kirks are also fascinating to study. Although monuments to prominent families were erected inside churches prior to the Reformation few outside grave markers have survived from before the seventeenth century. However, many old churchyards have some seventeenth-century stones and a wider range from the eighteenth century. Their variety of style and decoration is considerable. As well as upright stones there are recumbent slabs, table tombs where the slab is raised on legs and chest tombs where the sides of table tombs have been filled in by slabs. Decoration emphasises the emblems of death, a grim warning

Plate 22 The parish church at Lyne, near Peebles. A simple but attractive example of a post-Reformation kirk, dating from the 1640s

Plate 23 A finely-decorated table tomb from the churchyard at Tranent

Plate 24 A tombstone from Pencaitland. The grim symbols of mortality are carved above the tools of the deceased man's trade

to those still alive, and also in many cases the tools of the deceased person's trade. Sometimes these are easy to identify like the scissors of the tailor or the hammer of the smith. In other cases they are less obvious like the square and compass of the mason and the mill rind, the piece of metal supporting the upper millstone, for the miller. The standard of carving on earlier examples is often crude but effective. As the eighteenth century progresses the style becomes more refined and sometimes very elaborate. Among a wealth of churchyards one of the most notable is at Tranent which has a fine selection with some especially ornate table tombs.

5
CASTLE, TOWER
AND MANSION

ASTLES and towers are so much a part of the landscape of the
Lothians and the Borders that they deserve separate consideration. Throughout the medieval period and down to the early
seventeenth century conditions remained sufficiently unstable for
those who had the resources to build themselves fortified houses.
War with England encouraged this. Close to the Border, raiding
across the Tweed and the Cheviots was almost endemic even when
England and Scotland were nominally at peace. Local unrest,
including feuds like the particularly bloody and bitter conflict
between the Scotts and the Kerrs, also made it prudent for
landowners to shut themselves behind iron grilles and machiolated
parapets.

After the Union of the Crowns in 1603 the need for defence
declined: castle and tower gradually gave way to mansion and
country house. The transition was slow, due in part to lack of funds
for large-scale rebuilding until agriculture began to be more
profitable in the later eighteenth century. Initially many towers were
converted and extended rather than replaced. There was also
continuity in style. The first classical mansions did not appear until
the late seventeenth century and were preceded by houses in a
vernacular style built by local masons which were strongly influenced
by the earlier fortified houses. This chapter charts the development
of castles and towers and shows how they gave way to undefended
country houses.

MOTTE AND BAILEY

The settlement of Anglo-Norman families in Scotland during the
twelfth and thirteenth centuries under the patronage of David I and
his successors brought with it a new system of landholding –
feudalism – and a new style of defence. The colonists introduced the

motte and bailey castle, built of earth and timber, which had become the standard form of defence in England. Scottish mottes were similar to their counterparts south of the Border; an artificial mound topped by a wooden palisade and tower and defended by a ditch around the base. Attached to the motte was the bailey, a larger level area defended by a ditch, bank and palisade, inside which were buildings for storage and accommodation.

Although many Norman families received land grants in the Lothians and Borders comparatively few mottes have survived. There are hardly any in the Lothians and only a few in the Borders. They are more characteristic of frontier areas like Galloway and north-east Scotland where the new feudal lords required a secure base from which to control their estates. South-east Scotland was close enough to royal authority to be more easily controlled.

Nevertheless, some mottes were built and survive today. Other earth and timber castles, referred to in early charters or topographic descriptions, seem to have been obliterated. In some cases this was because mottes were later upgraded into more sophisticated stone castles. The site of the fifteenth-century castle at Borthwick in Midlothian was known as the Mote of Lochorwart and it is likely that the magnificent tower house which was built here has removed all traces of its more modest Norman predecessor. Historical records refer to a motte, now vanished, at Gladsmuir in East Lothian and the first castle of the lords of Dirleton, at nearby Eldbotle, traces of which have yet to be positively identified, was probably of earth and timber construction.

It was often unnecessary to build a completely artificial motte. Natural features could be trimmed and moulded with less effort. The motte at Riddell (520248) north of Hawick is an oval mound formed by shaping a natural ridge, surrounded by a bailey defended by a deep ditch and two ramparts. Some mounds were completely artificial though. The one near the centre of Hawick is a good example. Close to the confluence of the Tweed and Slitrig Water it has a classic inverted pudding-basin shape. Comparable sites are associated with the royal burghs of Peebles and Selkirk. At Peebles the motte was fashioned from a natural feature at the confluence of the Tweed and the Eddleston Water but the castle fell out of use at an early date and the site became built over. At Selkirk (470281) the motte is also a reworked natural mound. A more classic motte in open country is Castle Law in Berwickshire (814418). The motte stands nearly 8m (26ft) high above a steep slope falling to the Leet Water and is surrounded by a ditch 9m (30ft) wide and still 3m (10ft) deep. The motte is in the corner of a rectangular bailey whose ditch

Plate 25 The earthwork defences of Liddel Castle, overlooking a spectacular drop to the Liddel Water, are still impressive

and bank are only faintly discernible on the ground but show up clearly on aerial photographs.

The most impressive earth-and-timber castle site in the Borders is Liddel Castle (510900). It is located on a bluff with a steep slope falling to the Liddel Water. Two other sides are protected by small tributary ravines. The more open south side, away from the river, is defended by two massive ditches and a rampart. The entrance was on the west side, above the long drop to the river. The castle was probably the 'caput' or headquarters of an estate which was granted to an Anglo-Norman incomer, Ranulph de Soules, one of David I's followers from Northamptonshire. It seems to have gone out of use by the fourteenth century and was replaced by the stone castle at Hermitage.

What kinds of homes did the lesser gentry live in? A range of housing, corresponding to the smaller tower houses of later times, is missing from the landscape. Many undefended sites must have been obliterated by ploughing or later building. One must suppose that down to the fifteenth century many landowners lived in houses built of timber rather than stone with few defences as their dwellings are so elusive in the landscape today.

In England homestead moats are characteristic of many areas. Consisting of ditches and earthworks, generally square or rectangular, enclosing farmsteads or timber halls, they have been identified by the thousand and mostly date from the thirteenth to the fifteenth centuries. Their earthworks were more for protection against wild animals than a serious military defence. Similar features can be seen at a handful of sites in the Borders. The most interesting is at Muirhouselaw near St Boswells (631283). Here there are traces of two enclosures, the larger one some 67m (220ft) square, defined by a broad ditch 6–9m (20–30ft) wide with low banks on either side. The northern corner of the enclosure is occupied by a pond which seems to have supplied water to the ditch. At other homestead moats the ditch may have been dry as there are no traces of a water supply. Inside the enclosure at Muirhouselaw are the remains of two buildings which may have been contemporary with the earthworks. One is two-roomed with a curious double thickness stone wall. The other, squarish, may have been the base of a tower.

A handful of square earthworks which may have been homestead moats have been identified in the Borders, but Muirhouselaw is the only one with traces of buildings inside. Two examples are found in Liddesdale. The one at Florida (517908) is easily accessible, but part of the earthwork has been removed by erosion. The other, at Kirndean (532909), is more remote, but the walk is worth it as the earthwork is better preserved, about 30m (98ft) square, surrounded by a bank 5m (16ft) wide which was presumably once topped by a palisade. In other cases small stone manor houses may have been rebuilt and extended into more substantial castles at a later date. Hermitage Castle in Liddesdale, which in its earliest phase consisted of two two-storey buildings facing each other across an enclosed courtyard, was one. Hailes Castle in East Lothian seems to have been another.

MEDIEVAL BARONIAL CASTLES

No early stone castles, dominated by a central keep or protected by a simple stone enclosure wall, survive in this area. The great medieval fortresses of the Lothians and the Borders are more sophisticated castles of enclosure with high curtain walls strengthened by imposing towers and gatehouses, usually incorporating the accommodation which had earlier been located in separate keeps. Few baronial castles have survived in the Borders at all. Centuries of warfare, particularly the struggle for independence in the fourteenth century and the English invasions of the 1540s, led to most early stone castles being demolished. Even the sites of some of them are uncertain. An example is Oliver Castle in the upper Tweed valley which is marked by the Ordnance Survey on a low knoll at 099250. There is, however, nothing to indicate that the indeterminate humps and bumps on the ground are the remains of the castle which is documented as existing c1200.

The most impressive medieval castle site on the Borders is undoubtedly Roxburgh. The fortress was built on a mound of fluvio-glacial sand and gravel over 20m (66ft) high not far from Kelso (713338). The River Teviot protects the site to the south and a massive ditch defends the base of the mound on the other sides. However, although the site is imposing the remains of the castle are disappointing. Roxburgh Castle existed in the early twelfth century and seems to have been a castle of enclosure with a keep and a church but no remains of these are discernible today. Being so close to the Border it was frequently in English hands. While besieging it in 1460 James II of Scotland was killed by the bursting of one of his own cannons. In 1545 the Earl of Hertford rebuilt it as a modern artillery fortification. This English fort was demolished in 1550 under the provisions of the Treaty of Boulogne and the scattered walling which

Plate 26 Only a few stumps of masonry remain of the once-mighty medieval castle at Dunbar. The arch in the foreground carried a covered way across an inlet of the sea to the artillery blockhouse which was added to the castle in the early sixteenth century

is all that is visible today probably dates mainly from this time.

Next to Roxburgh, the most strategically important castle in south-east Scotland was Dunbar, guarding access to the Lothian plain by the coastal route. Unfortunately, like Roxburgh, its remains are not impressive today. On the clifftops overlooking the later harbour a few stumps of walling give a poor impression of its former size and strength. It was held against the English in a nineteen-week siege by the redoubtable 'Black Agnes', Countess of Dunbar, in 1339. As at Roxburgh most of the remains date from the sixteenth century rather than from earlier periods.

East Lothian has some more intact medieval castles. It is hard to appreciate the massive strength of Dirleton Castle (515839) at first because it stands in such a peaceful setting, overlooking a village green and surrounded by well-tended lawns. The site is a craggy outcrop which has been steepened by quarrying. The curtain wall on the western side has been removed almost to foundation level but the rest is well preserved. Its massive round towers, deep rock-cut ditch and drawbridge are the childhood epitome of a medieval castle. The first stone castle was built around 1240 by John de Vaux, *seneschal* or steward to Marie de Coucy, Alexander II's French queen. The de Vaux were an Anglo-Norman family from Cumberland but originated from near Rouen and John adopted the most advanced features of castle design from contemporary France. The castle consisted of three huge stone towers and two smaller ones linked by a curtain wall. Dirleton was a status symbol, an affirmation in stone of its owner's wealth, influence and success. After being held by both Scots and English during the Wars of Independence the castle was demolished to deny the English a holding point but was rebuilt later in the fourteenth century. The fortress last saw action in 1650 when one of Cromwell's generals besieged a band of royalists who were holding it.

The most striking feature of the castle today is the massive thirteenth-century drum tower from the first, de Vaux, phase of construction. This tower was effectively the keep, incorporating a hall for the lord of the castle above and accommodation for the garrison below. The foundations of the other two main towers from this period can also be seen but most of the castle, including the wing housing the first-floor hall with kitchens at one end, private chambers at the other and storage beneath, dates from the later fourteenth-century rebuilding.

Most impressive of Lothian castles for its magnificent setting as well as its air of impregnability is Tantallon (596851) only a few kilometres from Dirleton. Tantallon stands on a clifftop promontory

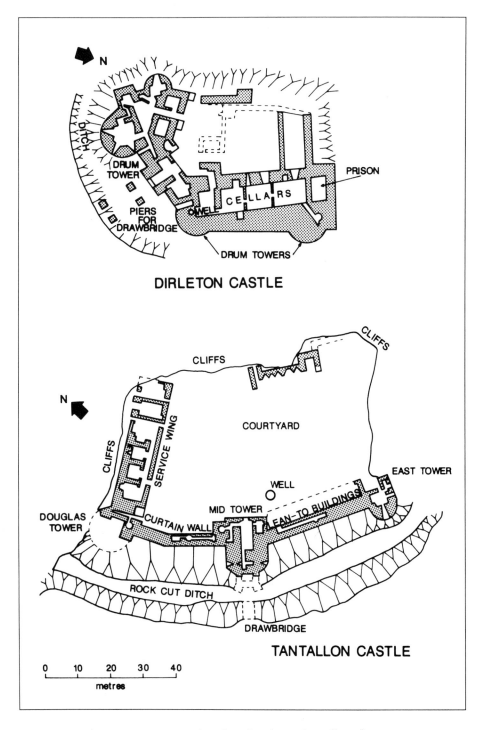

Fig 12 Two examples of medieval curtain wall castles

with a sheer drop on three sides, the crash of waves on the rocks below mingling with the cries of seabirds. The site is similar to Dunbar Castle but there has been less destruction and deterioration. Tantallon looks towards the rugged volcanic island of the Bass Rock and an old saying: 'ding doon Tantallon, mak a brig to the Bass' expressed two seemingly impossible feats. Indeed, before the period when its fortifications became obsolete, nobody did manage to 'ding doon' the castle. Even Cromwell's forces found the ruined castle a tough nut to crack in 1650: the garrison only surrendered after a twelve-day bombardment. In layout, Tantallon is a castle of enclosure with the defences concentrated on the landward side. The steepness and height of the cliffs made substantial defences on the other sides unnecessary. You approach it through a series of outworks including a great ditch with ramparts on either side and a gateway defended by a wall and tower. Beyond this is the bailey. Between this and the castle is a further rock-cut ditch. Above it rises the main façade, a central tower and two flanking ones joined by a high curtain wall of red sandstone, 4m (13ft) thick and over 15m (50ft) high. Tantallon was the chief stronghold of the powerful Douglas family and its impregnability allowed them to defy the Crown with impunity on more than one occasion. Both James IV and James V besieged the Douglases here without success.

Outside the Lothians the best preserved and most distinctive medieval fortress is Hermitage Castle at the head of Liddesdale. Its stark outline and remote setting give it a powerful atmosphere of menace and it is no surprise to learn that one of the de Soulis family, the original owners, was reputed to have been a warlock and was supposedly boiled alive by his enemies! The castle stands beside a stream surrounded by boggy ground which would have hindered the approach of attackers. There was a castle of some sort here in the thirteenth century but of this nothing remains apart from the surrounding earthworks. At the core of the present castle is a stone manor house which was probably built in the mid-fourteenth century when the area was in English hands. This building seems to have been badly damaged during the Border wars of Richard II's time and in the later-fourteenth century the Douglases remodelled the ruins into a tower house.

Then the castle was extended by adding large towers at the corners of the central block, with a particularly massive one at the south-west corner. Below the parapet, which is a modern restoration, you can see lines of holes. These carried timbers supporting a projecting wooden gallery or hoarding from which missiles could be dropped on anyone assaulting the base of the walls. This was later replaced

Plate 27 Hermitage Castle in Liddesdale, one of the best-preserved medieval castles in the Borders. The arch on the left of the castle allowed the machiolated parapet to be carried across the gap between the two towers. Below the parapet, holes for a defensive timber gallery or hoarding can be seen

by an overhanging stone parapet, pierced with machiolations, which served the same purpose without being a fire risk. On two sides of the castle, instead of running the parapet round into the recesses between the towers, it was carried across the intervening gap by masonry arches. These arches and the recesses behind them form the most distinctive feature of the castle.

TOWER HOUSES AND BASTELS

Great baronial castles are few in number in the Lothians and the Borders. Between the fourteenth and seventeenth centuries the normal residence for all but the greatest proprietors was a tower house. Tower houses developed in the fourteenth century when curtain wall castles began to go out of fashion. They were too expensive in a country impoverished by war: something cheaper, simpler to build, yet still defensible, was required. The tower house

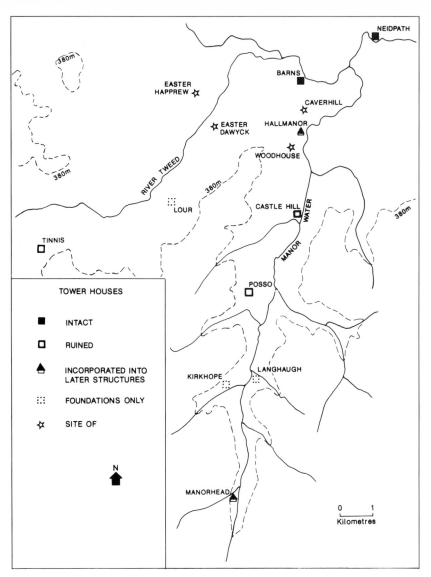

Fig 13 Sites of tower houses in the Manor Water valley

offered maximum security for a modest outlay. At the core of a medieval castle like Dirleton was a large hall with kitchens at one end, private chambers at the other and storage space in an undercroft below. The tower house took these elements and stood them on end – storage, hall, and the private quarters on top – within a thick stone shell which exposed the minimum ground area to attack. Their simple but flexible design could be adapted to the needs of both large and small landowners. Although they were only intended as protection against small-scale raiding they often proved formidable obstacles to larger forces.

Most towers were constructed in two main periods: the fourteenth and first half of the fifteenth centuries, and the later sixteenth century. Although defensive, they were primarily landowners' homes built in times of prosperity rather than war. Following the Union of the Scottish and English crowns in 1603 the danger of attack from across the Border faded, but many towers were inhabited until much later though their defensive role had ended.

Tower houses were ubiquitous; almost every proprietor with any pretensions built himself one. An act of 1535 required every landowner with a rental income of over £100 Scots to build a barmkin or enclosure with a tower inside. Many proprietors seem to have complied out of a desire for security if not respect for the legislature. There were over fifty in the old county of Peebles-shire and more than a hundred in Roxburghshire. There must have been several hundred in the Lothians and the Borders by the later sixteenth century and many can still be seen. Some are virtually intact. A few, like Borthwick in Midlothian, are still inhabited. Many lie ruined, either alone in open country or adjacent to the farmsteads that have been built from their robbed stonework. Some, cut down in size, have been turned into farm buildings. One at Flemington, north of Peebles (167452), is now a cowshed and can only be distinguished from the rest of the farmstead by its rougher stonework. Large numbers have vanished entirely or have left only a few heaps of stone to mark their location. In Castleton parish in Liddesdale, a frontier zone where raiding continued into the earliest years of the seventeenth century, there are no intact towers yet the Ordnance Survey marks the sites of at least twenty. A combination of English raids and the later re-use of their stonework explains their disappearance.

Tower houses were built to a fairly standard pattern. The basic design was simple and conservative with limited scope for variation and embellishment. Much of the fascination in visiting them lies in identifying the features of site, plan, and style which make each tower distinctive. Many simple towers had three storeys. The lowest was sealed by a stone vault, possibly with further vaults above. The basement storage area often had no direct communication with the upper floors save for a small hatch or 'murder hole' in the vault. Sometimes the main entrance was at first-floor level as an additional defence, as at Stoneypath in East Lothian (597714). Where the entrance was on the ground floor it was barred by a strong wooden door and an iron grille or 'yett'.

The main staircase in many towers ran only to the first floor.

Higher floors were reached by a separate stair corbelled out in a turret from the opposite side of the hall, another feature designed to hinder attackers. The turnpike stairs in such towers normally turned to the right. This meant that right-handed attackers trying to force their way up had their sword arms trapped against the well of the staircase while right-handed defenders, cutting downwards, had room to swing their weapons. Above the private rooms was a parapet walk and often additional accommodation in an attic room. The defences of tower houses were largely passive. There were few openings in the walls and the main way in which attackers could be threatened was from the parapet which usually projected outwards on corbels with gaps or machicolations through which missiles could be dropped on anyone attacking the base of the walls.

Towers were generally surrounded by a stone wall or barmkin enclosing a courtyard with the tower on one side and ranges of outbuildings on the others. If, in a sense, the tower was a poor man's version of the medieval keep then the barmkin was a scaled-down curtain wall. Barmkins around smaller towers were simple enclosures but those surrounding larger towers like Borthwick or Dalhousie were major defensive outworks with parapet walks, gun loops, towers and gatehouses.

Barmkins provided refuge for livestock in time of danger but the courtyard and outbuildings were expendable and the defenders would abandon them and retreat into the tower if necessary. Many barmkins have been removed in later landscaping operations but those at Newark Castle in Yarrow, Borthwick in Midlothian and at Neidpath Castle near Peebles are well preserved. Barmkins and outbuildings can also be traced around ruined towers. At Posso (200322), south of Peebles, the outbuildings are quite well preserved, with earthworks which were probably once an ornamental garden and orchard.

There are plenty of examples of smaller tower houses, unadorned square or rectangular blocks, which continued to be built into the late sixteenth century, Johnscleuch, deep in the Lammermuirs (631664), still in use as a farmhouse, is a simple rectangle with a semi-circular tower staircase protruding from one of the side walls. However, other towers were larger and more impressive with more complex internal layouts. Neidpath, built in the late fourteenth century, is an early L-plan tower. A wing added to the main block allowed a kitchen to be built adjoining the hall. Borthwick, constructed in the 1430s, immense in size and beautifully built of dressed stone rather than the usual rubble masonry, is one of the most impressive late-medieval castles in Britain. Little altered, apart

Plate 28 Neidpath Castle, near Peebles, an intact example of an early L-plan tower house

from some damage inflicted by Cromwell's forces, it is still inhabited. It has a rectangular main block with two parallel wings on one side. On the first floor this arrangement allows a hall with an adjoining kitchen in one wing and a solar, or private apartment, in the other. The walls are over 4m (13ft) thick and each of the four floors is vaulted. The original entrance was on the first floor, reached by a flying bridge from the surrounding curtain wall, and protected by a guard chamber in the recess of the wall.

Larger towers had thicker walls and higher vaults. Sometimes extra timber floors were inserted between the vaults to increase the number of rooms. The desire for more space led to more elaborate layouts although the range of permutations was small. The problems of defending a simple square tower, particularly with the development of firearms, also encouraged developments in plan. A common one, adopted early at Neidpath, was an L-shape with the main entrance placed in the re-entrant angle between the main block and a wing. In later examples this allowed the entrance to be covered by flanking gun loops. The double-L plan at Borthwick has already been mentioned. Even more sophisticated was the Z-plan where two towers or wings were placed at opposite corners of the main block containing gunloops which provided enfilading fire along all the walls. Nunraw (589707) in East Lothian is an example. At Preston Tower (379739) the problem of lack of space was solved by constructing two additional storeys above the original parapet walk producing a double-decker tower with a top-heavy appearance.

Many small landowners could not afford tower houses and there may have been a class of cheaper, simpler defensive structures in the Borders which has not so far been recognised in any numbers. In Northumberland there are many examples of *bastel* houses (from the French 'bastille'), rectangular two-storey farmhouses with vaulted ground floors for livestock and storage and first-floor entrances leading into single multi-functional rooms, poorer versions of the tower house's hall. In Northumberland these houses, which provided basic protection against small-scale raiding, were often inhabited by more well-to-do farmers. They also existed on the Scottish side of the Border during the troubled years of the mid-sixteenth century. The village of Lessudden had sixteen in 1544. Remarkably few have been identified in the modern landscape though. Fairnington House (644280) near Roxburgh is mainly late seventeenth century in date but a wing incorporates a sixteenth-century rectangular *bastel*. Queen Mary's House in the centre of Jedburgh is a more impressive example. It is a three-storey rectangular house with a square tower in the middle of one side and a corbelled stair tower in the one of the angles between the tower and the main block. Probably built in the late sixteenth century, it has clear affinities with contemporary tower houses but it has crow-stepped gables rather than a parapet and seems originally to have been thatched.

At an even lower level of sophistication and defensive capability is an interesting group of buildings south of Jedburgh among the rolling foothills of the Cheviots. They have been called '*pele* houses' but there is no sharp dividing line between them and *bastels*. Best preserved is one at Mervinslaw (671117) which, although roofless, still has its walls intact. It is a small rectangular building, two storeys high with gable ends and a garret. The walls are a mere 1.2m (4ft) thick but they have few openings. There were only two rooms: a storage area on the ground floor and a separate room above entered by an external ladder or stair. There was no stone vault but entrances to both apartments were barred by stout inner and outer doors. The house had no fireplace, suggesting that it was only a temporary refuge, and foundations of other buildings adjacent to it, set within an enclosure, are probably those of a farmstead.

Three other *pele* houses are situated within a few kilometres of Mervinslaw; no other certain examples of *pele* houses and very few *bastels* have been identified in the Borders. However, the recent discovery of a group of *bastel* houses in upper Clydesdale suggests that they may have been more common in the Borders than has been suspected. Many indeterminate ruins which have been considered to be the foundations of small towers may actually have been *bastels* or *pele* houses. Others may have been incorporated into later buildings; the lower part of one possible *bastel* lies within the structure of the Tontine Hotel in Peebles High Street. Being smaller and more flimsy than towers they would have been more easily demolished: many sheepfolds and corners of fields may hold surprises if examined more closely!

RENAISSANCE INFLUENCES IN CASTLE DESIGN

By the end of the sixteenth century new influences in castle design were leading to experiments in plan and decoration. That castles were increasingly viewed as homes, with defence a secondary consideration, is evident from the introduction of larger windows, the abandonment of parapets and the fact that gun loops were sometimes placed where they were more ornamental than useful. The contrast between older and newer styles can be seen at two neighbouring towers in the Merse. Smailholm (638347) on one hand, dating from the fifteenth century, is grim and blank walled, more like a prison than a home. Greenknowe (643384) on the other hand, built in 1581, has more and larger windows, an attractively corbelled stair tower and turrets, and a wealth of other embellishments and decorative features.

On a larger scale, Drochil Castle (162435), beside the Lyne Water, has a highly distinctive layout. Technically it is a Z-plan tower house but the square main block is so disproportionately large that it reduces the impact of the towers at opposite corners. Built for the

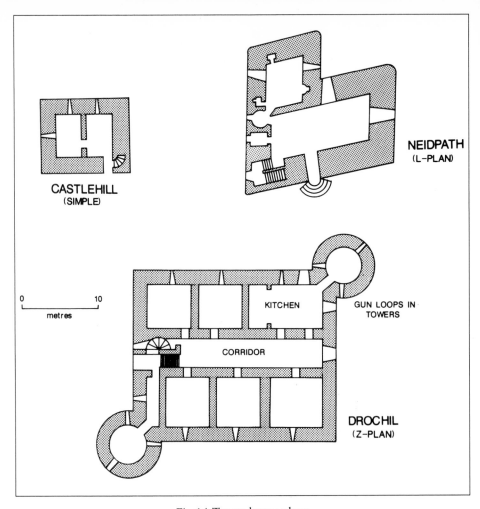

CASTLEHILL
(SIMPLE)

NEIDPATH
(L-PLAN)

KITCHEN

CORRIDOR

GUN LOOPS IN
TOWERS

DROCHIL
(Z-PLAN)

0   10
metres

Fig 14 Tower house plans

fourth Earl of Morton in the later sixteenth century, the main block is divided in two by a long corridor giving access to separate, self-contained rooms on either side. The normal pattern was for all rooms on any floor of a tower to open one into the other providing little privacy. Drochil does not seem to have been completed; another unfinished castle of original design was Barnes (529766) on the slopes of the Garleton Hills. Started in the 1590s but never completed, the house was rectangular with large square towers at each corner. Similar towers were placed at the angles and mid-points of the barmkin walls but it is not entirely clear as to whether they were defensive or ornamental.

Some simple towers were expanded on a massive scale by adding new ranges of buildings which turned them into courtyard castles. For instance, Crichton Castle in Midlothian (380611), a late

Plate 29 Preston Tower, East Lothian. More space has been created by building extra accommodation above the original parapet

fourteenth-century tower, was extended in the fifteenth and sixteenth centuries. The exterior is plain and functional but this outward simplicity is deceptive: inside the courtyard the façade is ornamented by projecting diamond-shaped blocks of stone highlighted, on a sunny day, by a sharp contrast of light and shadow. This form of decoration is reminiscent of contemporary Italian palaces and was indeed commissioned by the fifth Earl of Bothwell after a visit to Italy. Craigmillar Castle, on the southern outskirts of Edinburgh, was extended in a similar manner within an imposing defensive curtain wall.

Although not strictly a castle, the royal palace of Linlithgow exhibits many features of the new architectural styles which influenced sixteenth-century Scotland. Its homogeneous plan and styling belie its early origins and complex development. David I had a manor house here in the twelfth century on a rocky promontory above Linlithgow Loch. In the early fourteenth century Edward I replaced it with a castle. In the fifteenth century rebuilding was begun and continued intermittently for two centuries, although the most important phase was during the reign of James V in the early sixteenth century. The result was a palace which, although still possessing parapets, gunports and guarded entrances, is a totally domestic building. It consists of four ranges with corner towers laid out around a square courtyard. The outer façades are severe in appearance but those facing into the courtyard have large, symmetrically placed windows which let plenty of light and air into the royal apartments. The setting of the palace, with the imposing burgh kirk beside it, is a memorable one, especially when seen from across the loch.

During the fifteenth and sixteenth centuries the development of artillery began to change the design of fortifications in south-east Scotland although it was often the outworks which were re-modelled rather than the castle itself, as at Craigmillar where a high curtain wall was strengthened at the angles by adding drum towers containing gun loops. Gun loops, usually shaped like inverted keyholes, through which arquebuses and small cannon could be fired, replaced apertures for archers and are prominent at Tantallon where the ramparts defending the bailey may also have been remodelled to soak up cannon fire and protect the base of the curtain wall. After the castle was surrendered to the Crown in 1529 the internal chambers in the curtain wall were filled up with stone to strengthen it against future bombardment. Beyond the bailey is a further artillery fortification, an arrow-headed earthwork called a *ravelin*.

THE FIRST UNDEFENDED MANSIONS

By the early seventeenth century, with the crowns of England and Scotland united and local feuding declining, the need for fortified houses diminished. Scottish landowners began to look at English and Continental country houses and to think about building more spacious and comfortable residences, Often it was possible to add extra accommodation to existing towers. Lennoxlove in East Lothian is a good example of how a medieval tower house could be remodelled and improved. A large extension was added early in the seventeenth century and redesigned with a more symmetrical façade some decades later. Undoubtedly the grandest of these transitional houses, part castle part mansion, is Traquair House south of Innerleithen. The original three-storey tower forms one end of the present main block. Extensions were added in the mid-sixteenth and seventeenth centuries to a height of four storeys and the tower was raised to match. At the end of the seventeenth century a courtyard, flanked by two service wings, was added in front of the house. Modifications in the eighteenth and nineteenth centuries tried to impose as much symmetry as possible on a complex, composite design. Traquair is a delightful blend of old and new architectural ideas and lifestyles. Thirlestane Castle near Lauder reflects a similar transitional stage. Originally a simple tower house, it was remodelled in the late-sixteenth century into a rectangular building with round towers at the corners, a layout that was advanced for the period. A century later the Duke of Lauderdale, Charles II's minister, employed the architect Sir William Bruce to rebuild the house. The result was a tall mansion with large windows yet retaining the towers, turrets and parapet of a castle.

Smaller undefended country mansions first appeared in the Lothians in the early-seventeenth century. Two houses in the village of Preston (389739) are good examples of this new style. Hamilton House was built in 1626 for a successful Edinburgh advocate. It consists of a main block with two wings framing a small courtyard. The original entrance is in a semi-hexagonal tower in the angle between the main block and the west wing. The plan preserves echoes of tower-house design in an undefended building. Nearby is Northfield House, built for a wealthy Edinburgh merchant. Its steeply-pitched roof with attic dormers and corbelled corner turrets recalls the main block at Traquair and it seems to be an older building, perhaps sixteenth-century in date, which has been re-designed. Like Hamilton House the original entrance was in a tower set in the angle between the main block and a wing.

The style of these early mansions was purely vernacular, using layouts evolved only slightly from sixteenth-century tower houses. Their main blocks were still rectangular, only one room deep, with all the apartments interconnecting. Extra accommodation was provided in wings producing L-plans reminiscent of earlier castles with tower staircases in the angle between the main block and the wing. Only slowly were symmetrical façades, central staircases, and double-pile arrangements two rooms deep introduced. Winton House (449696) near Pencaitland is possibly the best example of the Renaissance country house tradition in Scotland. Built in the 1620s, it has classical ornamentation including tall twisted stone chimney stacks which can be paralleled in many Elizabethan and Jacobean mansions south of the Border, but hardly anywhere else in Scotland. The use of ashlar masonry at Winton contrasts with the rubble masonry which was normal for houses of this period.

By the time of the Union a new style of smaller country house was starting to appear with unified and symmetrical façades, laid out around a central doorway, two storeys in height, sometimes with a sunken basement. Two East Lothian houses demonstrate this transition. Pilmuir House (486695) was built in 1624 and despite

Plate 30 Bankton House, Prestonpans, an early eighteenth-century mansion which reflects Dutch influences in its curving gables

later changes its steep crow-stepped gables have a definite seven-teenth-century air. The original entrance was in a central wing housing a stair tower, with a corbelled stair turret giving access to the upper floors in classic tower-house style. In the early eighteenth century the rear of the house was remodelled into a new front with a symmetrical façade and a new entrance in the centre approached by a flight of steps. The two faces of Pilmuir reflect different centuries, one looking back to the old fortified house, the other looking forwards to the Georgian mansion. Bankton House (395736) stands roofless behind a farmyard at Prestonpans station. It belonged to Colonel Gardiner, the Hanoverian dragoon commander who was killed within sight of his home during the battle of Prestonpans in 1745. A flight of steps leads across a sunk basement to the main doorway with a classical pediment and curving Dutch-style gables. By the mid-eighteenth century the Georgian mansion had reached a standardised design which, scaled down, served admirably as the home of a prosperous farmer or, expanded with wings or pavilions and an extra storey, as a sizeable country mansion.

THE CLASSICAL COUNTRY HOUSE

The first classical mansions, using designs developed by Andrea Palladio in Italy, and filtered through the work of English architects like Vanbrugh and Wren, began to appear in the later-seventeenth century. Their first exponent was Sir William Bruce, a gentleman architect who was a contemporary and admirer of Sir Christopher Wren. Much of his early work involved remodelling existing houses, like Lennoxlove and Thirlestane which were modernised for the Duke of Lauderdale. Bruce's other achievements included Mertoun (618318) in Berwickshire and Craigiehall near Edinburgh. His masterpiece, a completely new design, was Hopetoun House in West Lothian, built between 1699 and 1702 for the first Earl of Hopetoun. The Hopetoun family had made their fortune from the lead mines at Leadhills and they commissioned a design which was based on the most up-to-date houses south of the Border. It consisted of a central main block with side pavilions linked by screen walls to the main building. Twenty years later the Earl employed William Adam to enlarge the house on a scale which was grander than anything yet seen in Scotland. Using Bruce's central block as a starting point Adam remodelled and extended the house producing the imposing façade which can be seen today with concave walls linking two large pavilions to the extended main block of the house. In detail the two

Plate 31 Lauderdale House, a country mansion in an urban setting, dominating the main street of Dunbar. It was designed by Robert and James Adam in the 1790s

periods of work by different architects sometimes fail to match but the overall result was a splendid and impressive house which set a new standard for Scottish landowning families.

Despite the magnificence of Hopetoun, only a few new country houses were built in south-east Scotland during the late-seventeenth and first half of the eighteenth centuries. There was not enough money available and most landowners adapted and extended their traditional fortified houses. Bruce's classical tradition was continued by architects like James Smith who remodelled the rambling mansion of Dalkeith into a more unified layout, rebuilding the front and adding pavilions and wings. William Adam, who died in 1748, was the last architect to have a distinctively Scottish classical style. Apart from Hopetoun, his achievements included Yester House (544672) and Mavisbank near Edinburgh.

The great age of rebuilding of country houses, coinciding with the peak of prosperity in agriculture which provided much of the capital, extended from the later-eighteenth century into the Victorian era. Foremost among architects in the earlier part of this period was Robert Adam. Among the houses he designed in this area are Newliston in West Lothian and Lauderdale House, a country mansion in an urban setting, dominating the main street of Dunbar.

Scottish and English country house design converged as architects worked on both sides of the Border. The Palladian style gave way to two broad types of design, the more purely classical, exemplified by Whittinghame House (606734) and the Georgian Gothic and Picturesque. A principal element of the Gothic revival was the castellated style. In a sense, with the remodelling of existing castles, the Scots baronial style was never out of fashion, but it was recreated for contemporary tastes by taking the plan of the Palladian mansion and embellishing the exterior with battlements, turrets and other military features. One of the first of these mock-castle designs was Robert Adam's Seton House in East Lothian, along with two Berwickshire houses which he designed, Mellerstain (647390) and Wedderburn just outside Duns. The tradition continued under other architects producing mansions like Tyninghame House, Stobo Castle, Melville Castle and, grandest of all, Floors Castle outside Kelso. Floors was remodelled in the mid-nineteenth century from a plain Georgian mansion built in 1718 for the first Duke of Roxburghe. It has battlements, towers, parapets, and pepper-pot turrets, with huge side pavilions in the same style framing the main block. One of the largest country houses in Britain still to be inhabited, Floors is palatial in scale.

Other early architectural styles were ransacked for ideas, including Tudor, as at Dalmeny House (168780), Norman and Gothic. Although not a grand country mansion on the scale of Floors, the house which epitomises so much of this architectural and intellectual movement is Abbotsford (508342), built for that arch-romantic Sir Walter Scott. The site was acquired by Scott in 1811 and the house was built from scratch, a Romantic extravaganza on a small scale whose fabric incorporates masonry collected from various historical sites in the Lothians and the Borders. The building of country houses continued into the early-twentieth century at Manderston, near Duns, where the original Georgian mansion from the 1790s was renovated and extended. The fine Edwardian kitchens, servants' quarters and dairy, which are open to the public, give a good impression of what life below stairs was like in an Edwardian country house.

6

THE LANDSCAPE OF IMPROVEMENT

THE pace of change in the countryside accelerated in the later-seventeenth century. Growing contact with England after the Union of 1707 led to more Scottish landowners appreciating the backwardness of agriculture on their estates compared with south of the Border. A few proprietors, more enthusiastic and far-sighted than their neighbours, began improvements early in the eighteenth century. In a country which was still comparatively poor, there was not enough money to finance large-scale changes before the third quarter of the eighteenth century. Then, with faster population growth increasing the demand for foodstuffs and pushing up prices, agriculture began to change rapidly. Starting in the 1760s the so-called 'Agricultural Revolution' transformed the countryside of the Lothians and the Borders within a couple of generations.

This area was in the forefront of improvement and in the Merse and East Lothian the landscape of improvement is at its most developed, a pattern of regular fields enclosed by hedges and stone dykes, interspersed with plantations of trees and large, efficiently laid out farmsteads. In the uplands too farming, and the appearance of the countryside, was drastically altered. The thousands of miles of march dykes, marking the boundaries of farms and estates, which follow the ridges or cross the valleys, are a testimony to the tremendous amount of labour and capital which was expended in the process of improving land which was often marginal in quality.

Although the outlines of this transformation are well known there have only been a few detailed studies of how the pre-Improvement landscape was altered. This is partly because the landscape which was swept away is not well recorded in either documents or old maps. Much of the work of change went on quietly within individual estates and did not generate the detailed documentation and maps which characterised English Parliamentary Enclosure which was proceeding at the same period. In particular, changes in the

Plate 32 Clearance cairns in fields on the slopes of White Meldon, near Peebles. The density of the cairns and the size of the boulders show how much effort has been made to remove stones from the improved land in a rather marginal location

seventeenth and early-eighteenth centuries have probably been underestimated because they have been less well publicised. This chapter looks at the new highly rational and efficient rural landscape which emerged from the later-seventeenth to the early-nineteenth centuries and at some of the ways in which it was created.

THE FIRST IMPROVERS: PLANTING THE POLICIES

In the late-seventeenth century the landscape of much of the Lothians and Borders was open and treeless. One of the first signs of change was the fashion for extending and embellishing the 'policies' or parklands around country houses by enclosing them into parks and planting blocks of woodland. Sometimes the *mains* or home farm was enclosed too and proprietors experimented tentatively with new agricultural techniques. They fattened cattle in their parks and imported English animals for breeding to improve the quality of their livestock. They also tried new crops and rotations.

These new enclosed policies were only islands of improvement in a sea of open-field cultivation and unenclosed pasture but it was a start nevertheless. One of the earliest parks was at Lennoxlove (515721). The story is that the Duke of Lauderdale had it built in

1681 for a visit to Scotland by the Duke of York, later James II & VII. On a previous trip to Scotland James had claimed that there were not 400 acres enclosed in the entire country. Lauderdale, determined to prove otherwise, had 400 acres surrounded by a stone wall! However, the second Earl of Tweeddale was already creating a more extensive park at Yester. The policies around Yester were probably the largest in Scotland at the end of the seventeenth century. A description of the estate, written about 1720, stated that the perimeter of the plantations was 13km (8 miles) in circumference and protected a million mature trees. This may be an exaggeration but the scale of planting was undoubtedly unique and John Adair's map of East Lothian, drawn in the 1690s, shows the policies at Yester as huge compared with those on other estates in the county.

Perhaps the most famous early improver was the sixth Earl of Haddington. At Tyninghame, in the first years of the eighteenth century, he began to enclose land and lay out plantations, often on sandy coastal soils which his neighbours considered too poor to improve. He placed shelter belts of trees around his new enclosed parks to protect them from the salt sea winds and also planted larger blocks of woodland. The Binning Wood, a 162ha (205 acre) block, was the most celebrated, particularly as it contained a lot of beech trees which at the time were rare in Scotland. The woods were not merely ornamental though: they were big business. The Earl of Haddington received a regular income from the thinnings and later, when the trees were mature, a sawmilling industry grew up at Tyninghame: the water-powered sawmill still survives in the village. The earl was also one of the first landowners in Scotland to experiment with fallowing his arable land and trying new crops like clover and sown grasses, to the ridicule of less progressive neighbours who couldn't see the sense of sowing grass on land that could produce a crop of corn.

Improving the policies and even enclosing the home farm was all very well but the overall impact of this work was limited. A start was needed on improving standards of farming throughout each

(opposite above) Mitchell's Close, Haddington

(below) Moray Place in Edinburgh's New Town: perhaps the most imposing private residences in the city

(overleaf) The New Town of Edinburgh seen from the castle across the intervening valley which once held the Nor Loch and is occupied today by Princes Street Gardens *(BTA/ETB)*

estate. The tenant farmers were too conservative, and too lacking in capital, to initiate improvements themselves so the lead had to come from their landlords. The first landowner in the Lothians to remodel his entire estate was John Cockburn of Ormiston. He was an ardent Anglophile, a supporter of the Union of 1707 who sat as member for Haddington in the new Westminster Parliament. Contact with England had made him painfully aware of the shortcomings of Scottish agriculture. He wanted to help drag Scotland into the modern world and he resolved to introduce English farming methods on to his estate when he succeeded his father in 1714.

He began by granting long leases on favourable terms to tenants who agreed to begin enclosing their farms with hedges and ditches. Starting with four farms on relatively poor soils, he had the steadings on his estate rebuilt along more efficient lines. He also rebuilt the village of Ormiston and founded an agricultural society there for local landowners and tenants who were interested in improved methods of agriculture. Cockburn tried to initiate change for social as much as economic motives and in his enthusiasm he over-reached himself and went bankrupt. However, his work had attracted widespread interest; other landowners sent their best tenants to Ormiston to learn the new techniques that Cockburn had introduced and the best of his own farmers went on to make names for themselves as improvers.

The achievements of the early improvers are shown graphically in a map which is generally known as the 'Military Survey' or 'Roy's Map' after its chief surveyor, William Roy. Designed to provide Hanoverian commanders with accurate information about Scotland during the military occupation which followed the Jacobite rebellion of 1745, the survey was undertaken between 1747 and 1755. It was drawn on a scale of one inch to a thousand yards, and is in many respects the forerunner of the modern 1:50,000 Ordnance Survey map. In delicate water-colour tones it depicts the mid-eighteenth century countryside of the Lothians and Borders, picking out the enclosed policies and fields from the ridge and furrow of the infields and outfields and emphasising how much land still remained unimproved as rough pasture. In the most advanced areas, as around Haddington, perhaps a quarter of the land had already been enclosed but elsewhere the islands of improvement were still small and most of the landscape had probably changed little from medieval times.

(opposite) The skyline of Edinburgh from Calton Hill is dominated by the castle and by the later monuments of the New Town *(BTA/ETB)*

New Farms and Fields

Once the incentive and the capital were available arable land could be enclosed easily and rapidly. Where the land lay in runrig between tenants the proprietor could simply have the land re-allocated in compact blocks ready for enclosure with hedges or stone walls. Where holdings were too small to be viable under more commercialised management a proprietor merely waited until the various leases fell due and then refused to renew them, gradually consolidating holdings into larger units. Indeed, a gradual process of holding amalgamation had been taking place on the old multiple-tenant farms since at least the late-seventeenth century. The result was that many townships, instead of having half a dozen small tenants scratching a living, already had only one or two large holdings whose tenants worked them with the aid of cottars and farm servants. In upland areas like Ettrick Forest there had been an early amalgamation into large sheep runs in the seventeenth century. However, such farms had still needed to keep much of their more fertile bottom land under crop because of the difficulty of obtaining grain from the surrounding lowlands. This meant that much of the land that would have provided valuable meadow and winter pasture was tied up as arable and the size of the flocks that could be wintered was greatly reduced. As transport improved and a grain surplus from the lowlands was assured these farms turned their arable land over to producing animal feed, allowing them to increase the size of their flocks and to specialise wholeheartedly in sheep production.

Where different proprietors had their lands intermixed consolidation was harder, but another act passed in 1695 provided a straightforward means of dividing such land out of runrig. The most troublesome cases were large townships on former monastic lands where many sitting tenants had been granted their holdings in perpetuity and the old pattern of intermingled strips had been fossilised. For instance, the runrig lands of Eyemouth, which were divided in 1764, extended to 372ha (920 acres) broken up into over 600 parcels. Many divisions were arranged privately without involving the courts and have left few records. Other cases were more contentious like the division of the runrigs of Tranent. Here, around 200ha (500 acres) was shared between twenty-six smallholders. The rest was owned by the York Buildings Company which had acquired them as part of the estates of the Earl of Winton when they were forfeited and sold after the Jacobite rebellion of 1715. Disputes between the smallholders and the company delayed the division proceedings more than a decade.

A lot of the lands which lay runrig between tenants were consolidated quietly and without fuss in the middle decades of the eighteenth century. The new enclosures were usually rectangular rather than square. They were larger on lighter soils, often between 12ha (30 acres) and 20ha (50 acres), smaller on heavier clays where they were commonly between 6ha (15 acres) and 12ha (30 acres). The new field patterns were imposed on the landscape with a desire for precise order and regularity which was sometimes too rigid. On some estates grids of fields were laid out with little regard for important variations in topography and drainage. The new enclosed fields were bounded by hedges in parts of the lowlands but even here drystone dykes were often built from stones removed from the fields. Hawthorn was the normal hedging plant because it was quick-growing and sturdy but in some areas other shrubs were used. On the Marquis of Tweeddale's estates around Gifford beech was often planted for hedging. In some cases the hedges were allowed to grow beyond their normal height and huge close-set ranks of beech trees have resulted.

In the uplands, where hedges would not thrive, stone dykes – walls – were ubiquitous. Where the glacial clays of the improved land were much encumbered with stones, thick consumption dykes were sometimes constructed to use them up. Alternatively, the stones were piled into large clearance cairns in the middle of fields: good examples can be seen above the Yarrow Water near Broadmeadows. Where boundary dykes were constructed above the limits of cultivation small quarries were often opened immediately adjacent to the lines of the walls. If you follow dykes up the hillsides you can often find shallow, overgrown quarry pits beside them. The dykes were built to a standard pattern, with two outer faces of stone and a rubble core. The two faces were bonded together by courses of 'through stones' and topped by cap stones angled so that they shed water and kept the core of the wall dry. These dykes, which are such a prominent feature of the Border hills, represented a tremendous investment in time and labour. Today the expense of maintaining them is often prohibitive and crumbling dykes have frequently been replaced or reinforced by barbed wire fences.

The new landscape of highly commercialised farming was organised around farmsteads of improved design. In the Lothians and the Merse the mixed arable and livestock farms were the largest lowland farms in Scotland, often running to hundreds of hectares. Their steadings and outbuildings were correspondingly grand. During the later-eighteenth century the simple farmhouses and outbuildings described by George Robertson (Chapter 3) gave way

Plate 33 Cart sheds at Beanston, East Lothian, with a granary above. The number of arches is a good indication of the size of a farm in this arable-orientated area

to better-built, more spacious and more efficiently laid out farm-steads. Only a few of these, built by local masons in a true vernacular style, have survived as most were replaced by even more impressive buildings during the nineteenth century.

Traditional steadings incorporated the farmhouse, barn and byre in a continuous row or in a random scatter. The new farmsteads were grouped around courtyards to minimise movement and increase efficiency. The stackyard, where the corn was stored before threshing, lay outside the courtyard to the west of the barn so that the sheaves got plenty of air and did not rot. Inside the courtyard cattle could be fed during the winter. A line of cart sheds faced into the yard, the number of arches being a good measure of the size of the farm. Above them were granaries with the threshing barn built on at right angles at the rear. Early ranges of outbuildings often formed three sides of a courtyard with a wall on the fourth but later designs filled in the fourth side with another range of buildings pierced by a high-arched entrance gateway.

At first farmhouses continued to form part of the ensemble. However, the dunghill at the door no longer fitted the farmers' new genteel image and gradually, as their wealth and social pretensions increased farmers had their houses, now elegant two- or three-storey buildings, located away from the outbuildings emphasising the social distance between them and their workers. The new farmhouses were often roofed with imported slate while outbuildings and farm workers' cottages were covered in warm red pantiles which were cheaper and became the standard replacement for straw thatch. Farmsteads in the uplands had more limited storage requirements with correspondingly fewer buildings. They are often sheltered from the wind by clumps of trees but frequently stand out at a distance through having their stonework whitewashed.

Most of the farmsteads which can be seen today date from the 1820s to the 1850s. These later steadings were architect-designed, often from widely-circulated pattern books. Although laid out on even more strictly functional lines than their predecessors, they were often more finely embellished. They were built during a period when farming had reached a peak of prosperity and farmers and landowners alike were prepared to spend a lot of money in improving the look of their farmsteads. Decorations included clock towers and dovecots while the architectural styles used varied from the severely classical, like the façade of Phantassie farm near East Linton (598773), through Scottish baronial like Sunnyside (595755) to Gothic revival.

The improvement of farm workers' accommodation lagged behind that for farmers and their animals. However, by the early-nineteenth century squalid cottar houses were beginning to give way to decently-built single-storey cottages with solid walls of sandstone rubble and pantiled roofs. Many examples still survive, often built in rows adjacent to the steadings which they served. In some parts of Scotland most farm workers were unmarried and lived a rough existence in communal bothies among the outbuildings. In the Lothians and the Merse, however, it was more common to employ married farm workers and to give them decent housing. Good examples can be seen almost everywhere but there is a particularly fine group opposite the station at Drem (510796).

The end product of all this activity was a highly efficient, rationally laid out landscape. William Cobbett, the celebrated English writer on agriculture and rural life, visited this area in the early-nineteenth century. He was impressed, almost over-awed, by what he saw. In the early-eighteenth century Scottish landowners had brought English farmers north to show them new techniques; now English landowners were bringing Scottish farmers south for the same reason. The transformation of the landscape, mostly accomplished in a couple of generations, was remarkable. Cobbett, looking at East Lothian, considered it 'land as fine as it is possible to be . . . Everything is abundant here except people who have been studiously swept from the land.' Indeed, the farmlands of the Lothians and the Merse do sometimes look empty and abandoned because of the lack of isolated houses and cottages between the farmsteads but Cobbett was mistaken in thinking that this was clear evidence of the landscape being depopulated. In fact the big new farmsteads and their attendant cottages often held as many people as small villages elsewhere. In addition, many people had settled in the new planned estate villages.

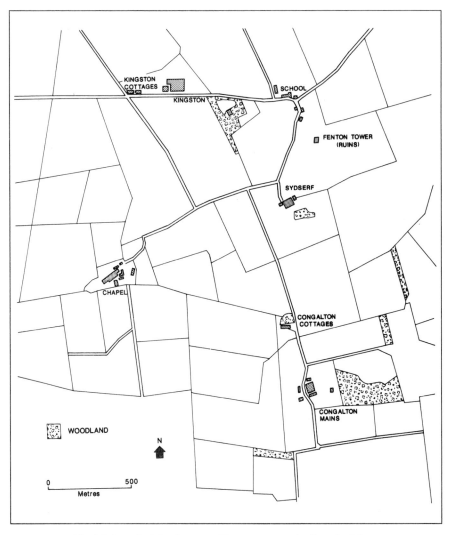

Fig 15 A typical landscape of improvement in East Lothian

126

PLANNED VILLAGES

Accompanying the transformation of the Scottish countryside in the later-eighteenth and nineteenth centuries were major changes in the settlement pattern. Over 300 new planned villages were established throughout Scotland. The aim of many of them was to develop rural industry, particularly textiles, to provide employment for a growing population not all of which could be accommodated on the land. The villages provided a market for estate produce and often developed as local service centres.

Planned villages are more densely clustered in certain parts of Scotland, notably the north-east. In the Lothians and the Merse it was less common for completely new villages to be laid out as the countryside already contained many nucleated settlements. However, some villages were re-sited and rebuilt while many others were given a facelift. The cottages in these estate villages are characteristically single-storey, sometimes with dormers. This emphasises the continuity in building traditions from the pre-Improvement era and distinguishes most Scottish villages from those south of the Border although the planned villages of south-east Scotland have a larger proportion of two-storey houses than those in other areas.

The Scottish planned village movement had its origins in East Lothian during the 1730s when John Cockburn of Ormiston decided to remodel Ormiston along the lines of an English village. He brought in an English land surveyor to lay out the new settlement and its surrounding fields. The result can still be seen in the wide tree-lined main street of the modern village, broad enough for markets to be held and closed off at each end by right-angled bends in the road. The houses were mainly built by their occupiers with Cockburn providing the materials but he stipulated that the dwellings should be of high quality, with two storeys, mortared stone and slate roofs, at a time when single-storeyed thatched cottages were normal. He also established various industries including linen weaving, brewing and distilling. At one time the village contained nearly 600 inhabitants.

Later in the eighteenth century other landowners who redesigned their villages did so to a set plan and had all the buildings constructed at their own expense to ensure uniformity. Tyninghame is the classic example of a village where development was rigidly controlled by the proprietor. The cottages, school and village hall were architect-designed and the layout of the entire community carefully planned. Athelstaneford provides an interesting contrast for here the development of each plot was left in the hands of the individual occupiers.

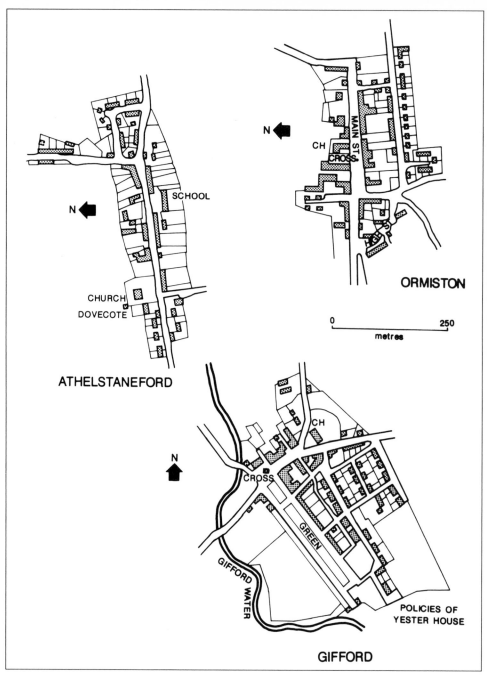

Fig 16 Some examples of planned village layouts

Plate 34 Tyninghame, East Lothian. A planned estate village where even the cottages were architect designed

The Kinlochs of Gilmerton leased off plots at moderate rents to people who would build good-quality houses to replace what the local minister called the 'small, dirty, dark hovels' which made up the existing village. Each landholder received a garden plus a share of arable land big enough for growing potatoes, or grazing a cow. This was a common feature of planned villages where most tradesmen were also smallholders. The result of each householder building his own dwelling within a general set of guidelines is evident in Athelstaneford today. The cottages are mostly single-storeyed, pantile roofed with rubble walls in a pleasant vernacular style with each house differing in detail from its neighbour.

Some planned villages were quite small, no more than a couple of rows of cottages like Carlops, 20km (12 miles) south of Edinburgh. It was founded in 1784 by the laird of Newhall, to promote the weaving of woollen cloth. The rows of single-storeyed weavers' cottages still stand on either side of the road. The Allan Ramsay hotel in the village, named after the seventeenth-century poet, was originally a wool warehouse. Nearby is Paties' Mill, the building which housed the original water-powered spinning machinery. When the mill ceased production with the advent of steam power it was converted into a corn mill and is now a private house.

Plate 35 Athelstaneford, an estate village where each occupier built their own house within a set of general guidelines, has a more homely appearance than Tyninghame

Plate 36 Newcastleton in Liddesdale, built by the third Duke of Buccleuch in the 1790s to encourage handloom weaving

One of the largest planned settlements was built for the Duke of Buccleuch in Liddesdale in the 1790s. The centre of Castleton parish, a hamlet of the same name, had been granted the right to hold markets and fairs in 1672. The Duke of Buccleuch had a site further down the valley developed on an ambitious scale as a weaving centre, naming it Newcastleton. It has a central main square and two smaller ones at either end. A minor street runs along the river roughly parallel with the main street, with cross streets between. The cottages, as in many other Scottish planned villages, are single-storeyed, designed in this case with large front windows to provide light for the looms. The way in which the cottages front straight on to the pavement without any gardens makes the village seem rather dour but this too is a common feature of Scottish estate villages. This layout was adopted because landowners feared that if the cottagers, who were often smallholders as well, were given space before their front doors they would use it for their dunghills, ruining the appearance of the model settlement!

Many other villages in the Lothians and the Merse, although not completely rebuilt on a new plan, had a lot of capital sunk into their improvement by their owners. In villages like East Saltoun the rows of plain single-storey stone cottages, with classical ornamentation around the doorways, are in the same tradition as the contemporary farm-workers cottages which were being built adjacent to the new farmsteads. At Dirleton there is an interesting contrast between simple cottages of this type dating from the late-eighteenth century and the much more ornate two-storey ones, decorated in the Picturesque style with tall chimneys, porches and ornamented gables, of a generation or two later.

Andrew Meikle and the Threshing Machine

The Agricultural Revolution in south-east Scotland was a triumph of improved organisation and innovation but few new mechanical inventions were involved. One new machine which influenced the landscape was the threshing machine. Although there had been several earlier attempts to design one the first effective threshing machine was produced by Andrew Meikle, a millwright near East Linton, in 1787. The first machine was produced for a farmer near Clackmannan but the second was installed at the farm of Phantassie, owned by George Rennie, a noted improver. His younger brother John, who served his apprenticeship under Meikle, became a famous engineer. Meikle's threshing machine could be driven by a variety of power sources. The most common method was horse power with two, four or sometimes six horses walking in a continuous circle inside a round or polygonal building attached to the side of the barn. These buildings, known as horse mills, horse gins, horse gangs or wheelhouses, are still common. It was the cheapest source of power to install but was exhausting work for the horses.

Other power sources were tried including water and wind. Water mills cost no more than horse gins but not every farm had a convenient stream to harness. At Crowhill (735741) the farmer was so determined to install one that in 1812 he had a 76m (250ft) long shaft built in a tunnel to transmit power from the water mill to the farmstead 20m (22yd) above the stream. The mill, shaft and tunnel still survive. Windmill-driven threshing machines were rarer as they were more expensive and prone to damage by sudden squalls. In the 1820s and 1830s, when steam power was being widely applied in factories, steam threshing machines became fashionable. The improvement of roads allowed coal to be brought cheaply to almost every part of the lowlands in the Lothians while Berwickshire was supplied with coal through its small harbours or carried overland from Northumberland. Steam driven threshing machines were only

Plate 37 This polygonal building attached to a barn near Dunbar housed a 'horse gang' for driving a threshing machine

Plate 38 Poldrate Mill, Haddington. A mill and granary on a site which has been occupied by grain mills from medieval times. Originally water-powered, Poldrate was later worked by steam

economic on larger farms. These were distinguished by tall brick chimneys rising above their outbuildings giving them the appearance of factories in the midst of the countryside, which in a sense they were. Although many of the chimneys have been demolished in recent years for safety reasons a considerable number survive. Beanston, near Athelstaneford (546763), is a good example as are Sunnyside (554755) and Luggate (596748) near Traprain Law. By the mid-1840s East Lothian had 386 threshing mills: 269 were horse-driven, 80 were steam powered, 30 were driven by water and 7 by wind.

7

MOVEMENT
IN THE LANDSCAPE

TRANSPORT and communications have been important to human societies from the earliest times but their legacy in the landscape of the Lothians and the Borders has been modest and difficult to interpret until recent centuries. Since the eighteenth century the growth of population, the development of commercial agriculture and the expansion of industry have created an ever-growing demand for transport. Technology has responded by providing improved systems of communication at an astonishing rate; stage coaches and turnpikes, barges and canals, steamships and enclosed harbours, locomotives and railways and, more recently, motor vehicles and motorways.

New transport networks have been created and then been replaced by further innovations. Many old roads, most of the railway network and a number of small harbours have been abandoned but are still prominent in the landscape and can be fascinating to study. Some old-established landscape features relating to transport are still functioning; several sixteenth-century bridges are still in use while express trains still thunder over some viaducts which were built in the 1840s. In other cases, lines of movement have remained in everyday use although the transport systems using them have been upgraded. Thus many modern roads follow the courses of eighteenth-century turnpikes while the main railway line from Berwick to Edinburgh and on to Glasgow still uses the route laid out by the first generation of railway engineers.

OLD ROADS

It is easy to take the modern road network for granted without thinking about how ancient some of the alignments may be. The story of routeways in this area goes back to prehistory but we can only speculate about the scale and nature of such early traffic and the routes that it took. Most of what is visible in the landscape relates to recent periods of heavier use. Nevertheless, by studying the course of routes on modern and old maps, and by examining their remains on the ground, it is possible to discover a good deal about the history of transport over the last few centuries.

Before the eighteenth century road transport was, as throughout Britain, slow, difficult and expensive. The price of a load of coal brought by packhorse or cart from mines around Dalkeith to Edinburgh, only half a dozen miles away, could be double that at the pithead. Because of physical difficulties and because the country was comparatively poor, few wheeled vehicles were in use before the eighteenth century except in the immediate vicinity of the larger towns. Most goods, including bulky items like grain and coal, were carried by pack horses. Over short distances sleds were often preferred to carts. Their lower centre of gravity made them safer on steep slopes. They were used for bringing peat down from the hill, stone from the quarry, or sheaves of grain from the fields to the stackyard.

Outside the towns most roads were merely bands of intertwining trackways worn by repeated use. They narrowed in at river crossings and between obstructions, like the policy walls around country houses, and fanned out through open country as each traveller chose their own path.

An impression of the character of these early roads can be gained by looking at surviving traces of them. The problem is to distinguish between the periods during which a particular route is known to have been used and the date of the visible features on the ground. For instance, the route over Minchmoor between Innerleithen and Selkirk is known from documents to have been used from at least the thirteenth century. The features that are most prominent in the landscape today are, however, more likely to date from the eighteenth century, the latest period during which the road was in regular use.

In the heavily-cultivated lowlands there are few traces of old roads; they either underlie modern ones or have been obliterated by cultivation. In more marginal hill areas, however, many old roads can still be traced. In such areas, as elsewhere in upland Britain, traffic tended to follow the hills rather than the valleys. The ridges were better drained and movement along them was easier than through the settled valley floors. In such terrain old roads often appear as terraces where they cross hillsides and as deeply-cut hollow ways where they climb steeper slopes.

A number of old roads cross the Lammermuirs. One, between

Gifford and Longformacus, runs parallel to the modern road and where it climbs Newlands Hill from 589657 to 596654 a belt of tracks up to 150m (500ft) wide can be seen with as many as sixteen separate hollow ways in places. Some are flat-bottomed and were probably cut by the passage of carts, others are V-sectioned and deepened by recent erosion. This route is mentioned in a thirteenth-century charter but the road was used as late as the eighteenth century and its present appearance probably reflects comparatively recent traffic. Another road runs from Longyester (545652) over the shoulder of Lammer Law. On the steep climb up the escarpment of the Lammermuirs the road appears as sets of terraces, often embanked at their outer edges. Once on top of the plateau of Lammer Law the tracks fade out in the peat. Other old roads cross the Lammermuirs from Dunbar to Lauderdale. The best known is

Plate 39 This deeply-hollowed track in the Tweedsmuir Hills was one of the branches of the 'Thieves Road' but was probably worn away mainly by the haulage of peat down to nearby farms

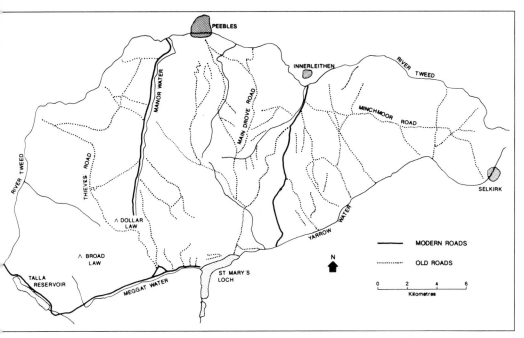

Fig 17 Old road networks in the Tweedsmuir Hills

the 'Herring Road' which climbs from near Spott over Lothian Edge, drops down to the Whiteadder near Johnscleuch, and continues eastwards by the head of the Dye Water towards the Leader. As the name suggests it was used in the seventeenth and eighteenth centuries by the inhabitants of the central Tweed valley to bring home pack horse loads of salt herring from Dunbar for the winter.

One of the most remarkable old routeways is the Thieves' Road through the Tweedsmuir Hills. It runs for many miles at altitudes of over 610m (2,000ft) with branches joining it from each side valley. In places it has merely been worn by use but some sections have been improved by careful construction. This is evident where the road runs along hillsides by the existence of drainage ditches on the up-slope side and revetments downslope, while steep gradients are tackled by carefully-engineered zig-zags. Although the name suggests that this route was used in earlier times the constructed sections were clearly intended for wheeled vehicles and are likely to date from the eighteenth century before the establishment of a full network of turnpikes opened up the surrounding valleys for carts and wagons and caused the ridgeway routes to fall out of use.

A specialised kind of road was the drove road. From the sixteenth century, reaching a peak in the eighteenth and early-nineteenth centuries, large numbers of Scottish cattle and sheep were driven to England to meet the ever-rising demand for fresh meat. Originally many of these animals came from the Borders themselves. By the later-seventeenth century, however, increasing numbers of livestock were being reared in the Highlands, sold to English buyers at great cattle trysts, at Crieff and later at Falkirk, then driven through the Borders. Some were sold in northern England to feed the populations of the growing industrial towns. Others were sent further south for the London market. By the end of the seventeenth century over 30,000 cattle a year were crossing the Border and in the eighteenth century the numbers rose far higher. The droving trade came to an end with the coming of the railways which allowed livestock to be transported far more quickly and easily than on the hoof.

From Falkirk a drove road led southwards to the Border. It crossed the Pentland Hills by the Cauldstaneslap pass from south of Kirknewton to the head of the Lyne Water. The route is still marked by the Ordnance Survey as 'old drove road'. Although millions of animals must have travelled this way over the years there is little on the ground today to mark their passage. The road continued south to the Tweed. Part of this stretch ran along turnpike roads: a high proportion of the revenues from the tollhouse at Romannobridge came from cattle. From Peebles the drove road climbed Kirkhope Law. Here it is at its most impressive because it is delimited by stone dykes. The walls were designed to keep the animals to a single line of travel and to prevent them from straying into the pastures on either side. Over the crest of the Tweedsmuir Hills the line of the road is only faintly marked. Where it comes down to the Liddel Water at Castleton (499896) it appears as a wide gap between enclosures while, on the opposite bank, a series of hollow ways climbs up from the river. The cattle were rested each night at regular 'stances'. Inns were often established near them to cater for the passing trade; droving was evidently thirsty work! A number of modern Border inns and hotels originated in this way.

BRIDGES

While road maintenance was often perfunctory or non-existent before the eighteenth century the problems posed by river crossings often led to the construction of bridges, the only significant form of investment in communications. Even here, compared with England, bridges were few and far between. The highly erratic regime of many rivers, notably the Tweed which was liable to sudden violent floods due to heavy rain in its hilly source area, worked against bridge construction. Between the destruction of the medieval bridge at Roxburgh in the sixteenth century and 1754, when a bridge was built

Plate 40 Now used only as a footbridge, this seventeenth-century bridge at Innerleithen was built using local funds to improve access to the parish church

Plate 41 Old Manor Bridge, near Peebles, built in 1702, was financed from the minister's stipend at a time when the parish was vacant

over the Tweed at Kelso, there was no bridge across this river between Berwick and Peebles. The new bridge at Kelso only survived until 1797 when it was washed away by a flood! Many early bridges were financed by burghs in the interests of improving access to their markets and fairs. The one at Peebles is a good example. The first record of a stone bridge here is in 1465 and there was probably an earlier wooden one in the same position.

The church was also a source of finance for bridge construction. The sixteenth-century Abbey Bridge over the Tyne downstream from Haddington may have been built by a nearby religious house and Jedburgh Abbey financed the fine sixteenth-century Canongate Bridge which still carries traffic across the Jed Water below the abbey. A number of fine bridges dating from the sixteenth century survive in south-east Scotland. The main road from Edinburgh to Berwick has good examples spanning the Esk at Musselburgh and the Tyne at East Linton while another crosses the Tyne at Haddington. In the seventeenth and eighteenth centuries, as the need for bridges became more widely appreciated, landowners often financed their construction. Old Ettrick Bridge, financed by Sir Walter Scott of Harden in 1628, is an example.

The great age of bridge-building in south-east Scotland was the later eighteenth and early nineteenth centuries. In Roxburgh and Selkirk alone twenty-four major new bridges were constructed between 1764 and 1813. Engineers developed flatter, broader spans. The newer bridges also incorporated hollow arches and piers which reduced their weight and allowed more delicate structures to be built without sacrificing strength. One of the grandest examples is John Smeaton's across the Tweed at Coldstream, opened in 1767. It has five main arches and two subsidiary flood arches. Even finer in its decoration is John Rennie's bridge at Kelso. Opened in 1803, it was the model for his later Waterloo Bridge and has pairs of Doric columns above the cutwaters. Another famous engineer, Thomas Telford, was also active in bridge-building in this region. Lothian Bridge across the River Tyne on the turnpike from Dalkeith to Greenlaw was opened in 1831 and is similar in style to another of his famous achievements, Dean Bridge over the Water of Leith in Edinburgh.

TURNPIKES

In the second half of the eighteenth century systematic road improvement began with the first turnpikes. These were roads improved using finance provided by groups of investors formed into turnpike trusts. Once the turnpiking of a stretch of road had been authorised by Parliament and the road had been upgraded, the trustees recouped their investment by charging tolls on traffic using it. The first road to be turnpiked, in 1750, was the Great Post Road from Edinburgh to Berwick, testifying to the importance of this route. For much of its course the road followed the line of the modern A1. However, a section of the road north of Haddington has been abandoned by modern traffic and can be walked or cycled in safety. From Cantyhall (434752) south-east of Longniddry the road runs eastwards as a farm track skirting the southern slopes of the Garleton Hills for over 7km (4 miles) until it reaches Phantassie (510757). Its gently sinuous course contrasts with the later, right-angled patterns of the fields on either side. From Phantassie eastwards the road vanishes although a curving field boundary among straighter enclosures probably marks its course. From Beanston Mains (553765) it continues as a cart track to Pencraig Wood (569765). Where the track turns at the north-west corner of the wood a short section of the original road, a worn hollow way, is preserved.

Other main roads from Edinburgh to Queensferry, Stirling and Glasgow were turnpiked in the 1750s. Another early turnpike led south to the head of the Tweed and past the Devil's Beef Tub to Moffat. Because of the severe upland climate this road was harder to maintain than lowland turnpikes, particularly as it was heavily used by carts from the Leadhills mines. Proportionately higher tolls were charged for using it. On the eastern side of the Pentlands between Carlops and Dolphinton you can walk a 10km (6 mile) stretch of early turnpike which has been almost abandoned by modern traffic and is perhaps the best unaltered stretch of one of these early roads in the area. The turnpike, now a farm track, leaves the modern main road at the south end of Carlops village. Following closely the line of a Roman road, it runs parallel to the A702 about ½km closer to the Pentlands. It crosses the Lyne Water upstream of West Linton, whose inhabitants were annoyed at being bypassed. Where the road crosses the West Water between West Linton and Dolphinton you can see one of the original bridges. A panel in the bridge indicates that it was repaired in 1899 but was first built in 1620. This indicates that the turnpike followed an earlier road, perhaps a medieval one on the line of the original Roman road. The turnpike was used until 1830 when it was replaced by a new one, now the A702, following an easier line through West Linton.

The turnpikes were so successful that in most cases they form the basis of the modern road network. Their former existence is

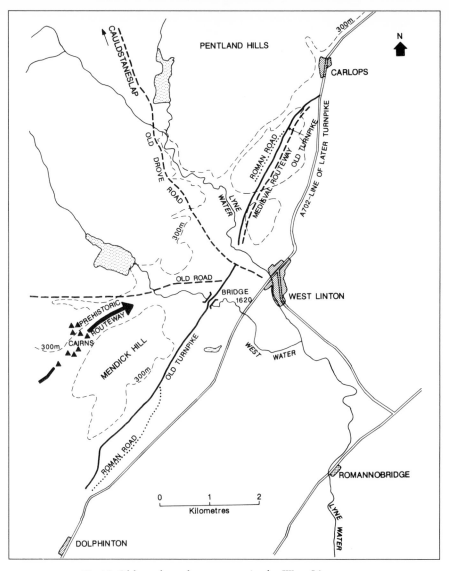

Fig 18 Old roads and routeways in the West Linton area

sometimes indicated by the survival of turnpike toll houses. These were generally single-storey roadside cottages designed with prominent bay windows to give the toll collector a clear view of traffic in either direction. Toll houses beside bridges can still be seen at Maxton and at Coldstream whose tollhouse was used for celebrating runaway marriages in a similar way to the smithy at Gretna. Where tollhouses have vanished, place names containing the element 'toll' often recall the turnpike era. Edinburgh has a ring of them such as Cameron Toll and Crewe Toll, marking the places on the outskirts of the expanding city where the turnpikes began.

HARBOURS AND HAVENS

It is easy to forget how important coastal transport was in the past but, given the difficulty and expense of overland transport, coastal shipping was vital to the economy of the Lothians and the Merse. Despite this, seaborne trade has always suffered from a lack of good natural harbours. Although many rocky creeks and some sheltered bays exist between Berwick and Bo'ness there are no good natural harbours of any size. Before the nineteenth century this did not matter greatly because cargo and fishing vessels were small and could operate from havens which were little better than open beaches. Ross, a few kilometres up the coast from Berwick, consists of a row of cottages at the foot of the cliffs with no harbour works at all yet its beach was used by lobster and crab fishermen well into the nineteenth century.

The increase in size of ships in the nineteenth century and competition from the railways led to the concentration of trade into fewer large ports like Leith and Bo'ness. This, and the decline of coastal fisheries, caused many small harbours to be virtually abandoned. As they have not been altered by recent port developments there is plenty of scope for exploring them and visualising what they were like in the past.

The simplest harbours can be the most fascinating. At Castleton (594850), below the cliffs on which Tantallon Castle stands, there are traces of a landing place which may have served a small fishing community as well as the castle. Just below the castle bailey an area of flat rocks is pitted with depressions which were the post holes for a landing stage. The date of this simple haven is uncertain but it was probably contemporary with the use of the castle, from the fourteenth to the seventeenth century. Beside the post holes is a channel in the rocks which seems to have been cleared of boulders to provide a safe anchorage for small vessels.

Several early ports were created by building quays along river mouths. Cramond, on the River Almond, is one which has remained almost unchanged. The Romans used the mouth of the river as a base for shipping and, if the reports of early antiquaries are to be believed, they may even have built a stone pier to protect it. In later times a quay was constructed on the east bank of the river. The harbour was a fishing centre but it also handled a considerable volume of trade. In the later eighteenth century a series of water-powered iron forges was established a short way upstream. The remains of some of them and the weirs which provided a head of water, can still be seen, while the factory manager's house is still occupied. The harbour was used

for importing iron and exporting the finished goods. Silting has affected the river mouth so that only small pleasure craft can use it today but a passenger ferry across the river still operates. The picturesque whitewashed cottages overlooking the quays, which originally housed industrial workers employed at the iron forges, have been attractively restored. These, with the old inn and parish kirk, make Cramond one of the most attractive minor ports along this stretch of coast.

Some harbours were built by local landowners to export the agricultural produce and mineral wealth of their estates. A good example is Skateraw (738754). The rocky creek here was used as a landing place in the sixteenth century but it was developed in the

Plate 42 The Victoria Harbour at Dunbar, built in 1842, is tiny by today's standards and only shelters a few fishing vessels

nineteenth century when it was realised that the local limestone could be used to supply agricultural lime to the area if coal for burning it could be imported. Two local landowners financed a small harbour with a limekiln beside it. The harbour is now derelict, having been destroyed by a storm late in the nineteenth century, but the limekiln remains to mark the site. An early example of landowners developing their own port was Morison's Haven (372738) where the monks of Newbattle Abbey received permission to build a harbour in the sixteenth century. They seem to have sub-contracted the work for the site became known as Acheson's Haven after the local man who had it built in 1541. A later landowner, William Morison, had it reconstructed and enlarged around 1700 from which time the port

145

became known as Morison's Haven. It served as the main harbour for the thriving coal and salt town of Prestonpans but reclamation of the foreshore has now filled it in.

In the early-nineteenth century the herring fishery was at the peak of its prosperity and a number of new harbours were built to accommodate fishing vessels, often at places which had been used by shipping for centuries but which had no proper facilities. Cove Harbour is a good example. A narrow road makes a steep descent down the cliffs to a rocky shore to reveal a hidden harbour. You reach it through a tunnel cut in the red sandstone. The rocks alongside are honeycombed with chambers which make one think of smugglers, though in fact they are more likely to have been used for storing or processing fish! There were no piers here before the eighteenth century. In the 1750s, and again in the 1820s, attempts were made to build a harbour, but the works were destroyed by storms before completion. The present harbour dates from 1831. The harbour at the attractive fishing village of St Abbs dates from the same period, but here the piers have been enclosed by later outer breakwaters to form a more sheltered refuge which is still used by crab and lobster fishermen.

During the eighteenth and early nineteenth centuries smuggling was rife, particularly along the Berwickshire coast which was rockier and more remote than the shores of the Forth. Redheugh (825703), 3km (2 miles) west of Fast Castle, was a notorious smugglers' haunt. A small natural harbour, awkward of access from the cliffs above, provided a secluded spot for landing contraband. You can still see iron staples fixed into the rocks for mooring boats. Smuggling ceased with the establishment in the 1820s of a coastguard station, on the cliffs above. The ruins of this, and of the coastguards' boathouse by the harbour, still remain.

Of the larger coastal burghs, Dunbar had one of the most important harbours. The earliest harbour was at Belhaven Bay, west of the town, sheltered from easterly gales by the cliffs on which Dunbar stands. The building of a proper harbour began in 1574. In 1655, however, a storm ruined the pier and the burgh received aid from the Cromwellian government to reconstruct it. The foundations of the present east pier therefore probably date from the sixteenth century. The old harbour reached its present form by the mid-eighteenth century with an extension to the east pier dividing the inner harbour from Broad Haven. Much of the distinctive character of the harbour today derives from the old buildings that surround it. Granaries and maltings act as timeless reminders of the fact that the principal export of Dunbar in the past was grain. Some of the warehouses around the harbour have been redesigned as flats with attractive new houses in traditional style between them. To the north-west is the larger Victoria harbour, built in 1842 and still quite small by modern standards, which is overlooked by the ruins of the medieval castle.

The Union Canal

In the later-eighteenth century, when canals were being constructed throughout the English lowlands and even across the Pennines, there was considerable enthusiasm for them in Scotland too. Unfortunately though, few of the projected schemes ever came to fruition. The indented coastline meant that few towns and industrial centres were far from the sea while inland the topographic barriers to successful canal construction were considerable. The most obvious route for a canal was across the isthmus between the Forth and Clyde estuaries. The industrial development of Glasgow had been severely hindered for years by its lack of direct access to the east coast. In 1775 the Forth & Clyde Canal was opened and construction of Grangemouth, a new outport at its terminus on the Firth of Forth, began. Bo'ness, Glasgow's early trading outlet to the North Sea, was threatened by the growth of the new upstart and went into a steady decline after the failure of a further scheme to link Bo'ness to the new canal with a branch.

The most obvious way of increasing the potential of the Forth & Clyde canal was with a branch to Edinburgh. This would allow coal from North Lanarkshire to be brought to the city and simultaneously enable grain from the Lothians to be carried to Glasgow. The Union Canal was completed in 1822 as a broad-barge canal. Fifty km (31 miles) long, it joined the Forth & Clyde canal at Falkirk and terminated in a basin on the west side of Edinburgh only ½km from the Castle. Running along the 73m (240ft) contour it conveniently required no locks but several aqueducts were needed to carry it over intervening valleys. The twelve-span structure over the River Avon is the longest and highest Scottish canal aqueduct but others still survive over the Water of Leith at Slateford and the River Almond at Lin's Mill. The water in these aqueducts was contained in cast iron troughs which were lighter than the usual clay lining and therefore allowed slender, more elegant structures to be built. Although it was closed in the 1960s and one or two sections have since been filled in, long stretches of the Union Canal survive, complete with their spectacular bridges, and providing interesting, attractive walks.

RAILWAYS: THE EARLY YEARS

The first railway in this region was a colliery waggonway from pits at Tranent to the sea at Cockenzie just over 3km (2 miles) away. It was built in 1722 by the York Buildings Company, a dubious group of speculators who had bought the Earl of Winton's forfeited estates following the failure of the Jacobite rebellion of 1715. The original waggonway had wooden rails with a gauge of 1m (3ft 3in). The loaded waggons trundled downhill under gravity with a brakeman to control their speed and the empty ones were hauled back uphill by horses. In 1815 iron rails were laid to replace the wooden ones. Part of the course of the waggonway can still be followed, cutting under the main road through Tranent at 402729 and descending the steep slope to the north through a gully known locally as The Heugh. The line of the waggonway has been landscaped into an attractive walk which emerges on to lower ground beside the old parish church of Tranent.

One or two other waggonways were built in the early-nineteenth century to serve collieries including one in 1814 from Pinkie to Fisherrow harbour 3km (2 miles) away. Waggonways were ideally suited to moving bulky goods like coal over limited distances but slowly the possibilities of using them on a larger scale began to be

Plate 43 The line of the York Building Company's waggonway from Tranent to Cockenzie, built in 1722, can still be followed for part of its route

considered. At their most expensive they cost only a third of the price of a canal and they were far more efficient than road transport.

In the early-nineteenth century many exciting schemes for longer waggonways were proposed but never developed such as one from Glasgow to Berwick through the Tweed valley. In the Lothians the most urgent need was for a link between Edinburgh and the coal mines around Dalkeith. Edinburgh's demand for fuel was increasing as the city grew and the standard of living of its inhabitants rose. In the later-eighteenth century most of the city's coal was imported via Leith. After the Union Canal was completed coal was brought by barge from North Lanarkshire and West Lothian but supplies were sometimes interrupted in winter by the freezing of the canal. There was plenty of coal within a few kilometres of Edinburgh but the cost of transporting it by road was so high that only small quantities were available. A start was made in 1818 with the construction of a waggonway from mines at Newton near Dalkeith to Little France on the southern outskirts of Edinburgh, a distance of under 6.5km (4 miles). A much more extensive network was needed, however, linking the city centre directly with a range of collieries but friction and mistrust between the proprietors of the various mines delayed this development.

Nevertheless, the growing demand for coal in Edinburgh led to the building of the first true railway in the Lothians. The Edinburgh & Dalkeith Railway was opened in 1831 but in its early years it relied on horse traction; locomotives were not used until 1846. The line started from a depot at St Leonards in Edinburgh, overlooked by Salisbury Crags, and ran around the south side of Arthur's Seat to Duddingston. This section of line is still clearly visible. From Duddingston it ran to the nearest pits at Niddrie and over the North Esk river at Dalhousie by a viaduct 18m (60ft) high. From here it was extended further south at the expense of the Marquis of Lothian, to develop coal mines on his lands. It crossed the South Esk on an even more impressive viaduct. A branch into Dalkeith was built for the Duke of Buccleuch to serve his collieries at Smeaton and Cowden. Another branch ran from Niddrie to the sea at Fisherrow and by 1838 the line had been extended round the east side of Arthur's Seat to Leith.

This line earned itself the nickname of the 'Innocent Railway' on account of its good safety record and because of the old-fashioned and unhurried way in which it was run. Notice boards warned drivers not to stop and feed their horses between stations! Despite its name this modest railway was a tremendous success. It moved over 300 tons of coal a day and a passenger service, started in 1832, carried nearly a quarter of a million people a year by the end of the 1830s.

The Innocent Railway was merely an extended colliery tramway which had diversified into passenger transport. The next major jump in scale was an inter-city link between Edinburgh and Glasgow, a distance of over 72km (45 miles). Fortunately the topography of the chosen route did not present serious problems and the Edinburgh & Glasgow Railway was opened in 1842. The line swung northwards through Linlithgow and Falkirk, running close to the Union and Forth & Clyde canals for much of its length, and is still the main inter-city link. Although most of its course was fairly level some river valleys had to be crossed. The most impressive engineering feats were the thirty-six arch viaduct across the River Almond and the twenty-three arch one over the River Avon. They were originally built with hollowed arches and piers allowing a slimmer, more elegant design, but in the 1950s the cavities were filled with concrete to strengthen the structure so that trains could cross them at higher speeds.

THE RAILWAY NETWORK DEVELOPS

Once Edinburgh and Glasgow were linked the next obvious target was a route across the Border. Many plans were put forward during the railway mania of the early 1840s. In 1844 Parliamentary approval was granted for the first trans-border line from Edinburgh to Berwick via the east coast; the North British Railway was born. It was the plan of the founder, John Learmonth, to annex a huge triangle of country between Edinburgh, Berwick and Carlisle but, like many early railway promoters, he was over-optimistic about the traffic that would be generated in this largely agricultural area with few towns or mineral resources.

Construction of the main line from Edinburgh to Dunbar provided few engineering problems as gradients were gentle, although bridges were required over the Esk at Inveresk and the Tyne at East Linton. Looking at the modern railway, which follows the same route, it may seem strange that the line runs north of the Garleton Hills rather than south of them through Haddington. At this early stage in railway development engineers still tried to avoid building embankments, cuttings, viaducts and tunnels wherever possible. The engineer who advised Learmonth suggested that to route the railway via Haddington, over higher ground, would add substantially to construction and maintenance costs. The solution was to build a branch line to Haddington whose inhabitants had in any case ambivalent attitudes to the coming of the railway. Some welcomed

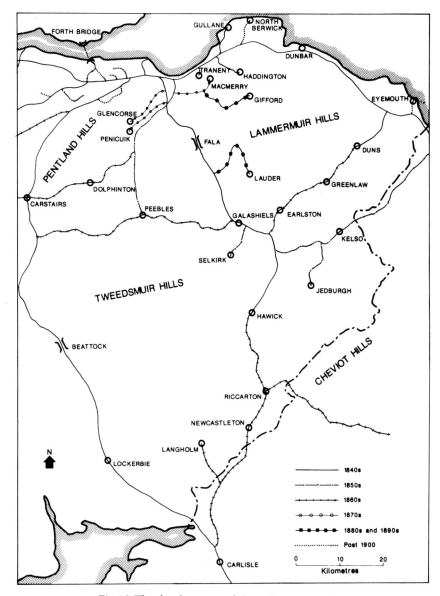

Fig 19 The development of the railway network

it but others, more far sighted, prophesied that it would undermine the town's position as the foremost grain market in Scotland once farmers could deal directly with Edinburgh or Glasgow.

Beyond Dunbar the character of the line changed with some difficult streams to bridge, like the Dunglass Burn, and a steep climb over the fringes of the Lammermuirs to Grantshouse. Nevertheless, the railway was opened in June 1846 and stagecoach services between Edinburgh and Berwick were immediately abandoned. The line had been built in a hurry with insufficient attention to potential environmental dangers. Parts of the clifftop section between Eyemouth and Berwick had been laid over old landslips and were unstable while heavy rain the following autumn demolished bridges and washed away embankments. A good deal of money had to be spent on repairs before the line could be re-opened. Despite this, some of the original bridges on the line are still in use, notably the six span viaduct at Dunglass and the bridge at Ayton.

So intent were the North British on annexing territory that they embarked on an ambitious but ill-judged programme of branch line construction instead of improving their main-line services. The branch to Haddington had originally been built double-tracked but traffic never warranted this and it was later reduced to a single track. Another line from Drem to the as-yet-undeveloped village of North Berwick was also built double track although only a single line was actually laid. The company had high hopes of generating traffic by encouraging Edinburgh businessmen to live in North Berwick and commute into the city. They introduced concessionary tickets to people with businesses in Edinburgh who had houses built within a specified radius of their stations. In time North Berwick did develop into a fashionable resort and commuting centre but initially revenue was so poor that in 1856, six years after the line was opened, locomotives were discontinued and the company resorted to horse power to reduce running costs. A branch to Tranent was more successful as it generated a lot of traffic in coal but another from Reston to Duns was a financial disaster. In an area where potential traffic was extremely small, it was folly to build a double-track branch line. This was soon realised and the line was reduced to single-track working.

Competition between railway companies to establish a route across the Border intensified in 1841 by a government decision that only one trans-Border line was viable. This proved to be an underestimation of the traffic potential of long-distance lines and by 1850 three Anglo-Scottish routes had been established; the North British Railway's east-coast line, the Caledonian's line from Carlisle to Glasgow via Beattock, and the Glasgow & South Western line from Glasgow to Carlisle through Ayrshire and Nithsdale. The North British, keen to extend their empire to Carlisle, received permission in 1845 for a line from Edinburgh to Hawick via Galashiels. The line, which climbed to over 275m (900ft) at Falahill and had to cross the Gala Water fifteen times, was opened four years later. The availability of cheap coal transformed the technology of the Border textile industries, allowing them to convert to steam power and expand their output. From this line branches were built to Kelso, Jedburgh and Selkirk in the 1850s and later to Peebles. By 1855 Peebles had already been connected directly with Edinburgh by a line via Eddleston and as a result of better access the town developed as a fashionable spa resort.

It was never the North British's plan for their line to terminate at Hawick. Their ultimate goal was a link to Carlisle. They did not achieve this until 1862 due to opposition from the Caledonian and lack of interest by the Duke of Buccleuch who owned much of the land south of Hawick. This line became known as the 'Waverley Route' because it passed through a region which had been popularised by Sir Walter Scott, author of the Waverley novels. The name was designed to catch the public's imagination and to encourage tourists to use the line. However, there was little hope that the thinly populated uplands between Hawick and Liddesdale would ever generate much traffic. The line was expensive to build with numerous embankments and cuttings, several viaducts and the 1.1km (0.7 mile) Whitrope tunnel on the watershed between Teviotdale and Liddesdale.

Operating costs on the Waverley Route were increased by steep gradients which required the use of two engines and the line was hard to keep clear of snow in winter. Nevertheless it was here that one of the most isolated railway communities in the country, Riccarton Junction, was developed, with rows of cottages, a school and a community centre. Standing on a bleak watershed between two tributaries of the Liddel Water, Riccarton was the point at which the Waverley Route was joined by a curious line, the Border Counties Railway. This line, opened at the same time, ran from Hexham in Northumberland over the crest of the Cheviots and was designed to exploit coal deposits at Plashetts, 48km (30 miles) north of Hexham. The Waverley Route was never a success as a long-distance route though the opening of the Midland Railway's Settle–Carlisle line in 1870 allowed direct trains from the Borders to London to be operated.

Once the two main lines had been built via the east coast and Hawick, a network of branch lines was established in the Borders to connect them. The Berwickshire Railway, completed in 1865, started from the North British terminus at Duns and ran for over 32km (20 miles) to join the main Edinburgh to Hawick line at Newstead. Long disused, its most attractive surviving feature is the elegant viaduct across the Tweed at Leaderfoot. Another branch line from Berwick to Kelso provided a second east-west link up the Tweed valley. These lines ultimately came under the control of the North British Railway.

Plate 44 The slender piers of the viaduct at Leaderfoot, on the former Berwickshire railway from Duns to Melrose, span the Tweed close to the modern road bridge

The Caledonian, trying to penetrate their opponents' territory, had a line built through the Biggar Gap to Peebles. They had also succeeded in establishing a line to Edinburgh from their west-coast route at Carstairs. This line is still in use, allowing west-coast passengers to reach Edinburgh across the bleak moorlands on the northern side of the Pentlands without having to travel via Glasgow. The Caledonian also tried to push a branch line along the other side of the Pentlands but only reached Dolphinton, a small hamlet which was distinguished by having two stations belonging to the rival companies.

In 1896 an act was passed encouraging the construction of light railways to serve remote and scattered communities. Because they were not expected to carry heavy traffic they were designed to be built and operated more cheaply than standard railways. The Lothians and the Borders were already well served by conventional branch lines and only two light railways were built but both of them are interesting. The first, opened in 1901, left the main line to Hawick at Fountainhall in the valley of the Gala Water and crossed the moors to the Leader Water. It was designed to serve the little burgh of Lauder which, although situated in a fertile valley, had been bypassed by the railway network. This route, long closed, now makes an attractive walk, winding through bleak country between isolated upland farms.

The last new line, also opened in 1901, was the Gifford & Garvald Light Railway which started from Ormiston but never got beyond Gifford. It ran through thinly populated countryside with few mineral resources and actually avoided villages like East and West Saltoun. Despite the improvement of roads during the nineteenth century the country south of Haddington was still relatively isolated. The line was promoted by local landowners hoping to open up markets for the agricultural produce and mineral wealth of their estates. Authorisation for the railway was granted in 1891 but squabbles between the directors and proprietors across whose lands the railway was to be built delayed its opening. One landowner, Fletcher of Saltoun, withdrew his co-operation and the line had to be re-routed in a big sweep south to avoid the main part of his estates.

As a light railway, the Gifford & Garvald was operated more cheaply than standard lines. Level crossings were unmanned; trains had to stop at them while the guard got down and opened the gates. The speed of trains was severely restricted and stations had only the most basic of facilities. The line had small hopes of commercial success; because it avoided so many villages passenger traffic was always limited. This was hardly surprising considering that it sometimes took nearly an hour and a half for trains to cover the 16km (10 miles) between Ormiston and Gifford. Even when services were improved in the 1920s it still took forty minutes to cover this stretch. Mineral traffic also failed to live up to expectations though the line was not a complete failure. It encouraged the proprietor of Wester Pencaitland to open a colliery there which employed up to 300 men and turned the settlement into a mining community.

The age of the train was soon over in this quiet part of East Lothian for the development of motor bus services in the 1920s killed off passenger traffic. Freight continued to be carried until 1948 when a flood swept away the bridge at Humbie. The line beyond Humbie was never re-opened though the western end continued to carry some goods traffic until 1962.

By the 1930s competition from motor bus services was undermining the viability of other branch lines and closure of the less profitable ones was inevitable. The lines to Dolphinton, Gullane and Lauder were all closed in the early 1930s. The flood of 1948 damaged embankments and bridges on the Berwickshire railway so badly that the line was never re-opened. Further closures followed in the 1950s with the lines to Duns and Selkirk being axed. Then came the Beeching era of closures in the 1960s culminating in the axing of the Waverley Route, despite much local opposition, in 1969.

The modern railway network is a very slimmed-down version of the one that existed a century ago. The main east-coast line, shorn of almost all its branches, the original route between Edinburgh and Glasgow, the branch from Carstairs to Edinburgh, and the line northwards across the Forth Bridge are the principal surviving elements. The sites of many disused stations are still clear; at many of them, including Innerleithen, Roxburgh and Stobo, the station buildings are still in use as private homes. The former station at Melrose, the only one surviving on the Waverley line, now stands incongruously beside the town's by-pass and functions as a craft workshop. Hundreds of kilometres of disused branch lines can now be walked, sometimes with diversions to avoid dismantled bridges, a sad but fascinating reminder of how quickly changes in technology can alter transport systems. The age of the steam engine is also over, although something of its atmosphere can be appreciated if you visit the Bo'ness and Kinneil Railway, a short stretch of line which recreates the Victorian era of railway travel with old locomotives and original buildings moved from other stations and re-erected.

The fact that many bridges and viaducts from the 1840s are still in use testifies to the skill of the early railway engineers but their most famous monument came later in the nineteenth century. The Firth of Forth had long been a barrier to integrating the railway network of south-east Scotland with the north, involving long detours or the use of ferries across the narrows at Queensferry or from Granton to Burntisland. In the 1880s the Forth Railway Bridge, 2.5km (1.6 miles) long, was built across the gap, using the island of Inch Garvie as a convenient stepping stone. With its three immense double-cantilever spans and the slender stone piers of its high approach viaducts it is one of the most distinctive bridges in the world. Its massive solidity was due to caution by its designers following the Tay Bridge disaster of 1879. Nothing typifies better the ability of nineteenth-century railway engineers to overcome topography and master the physical environment than this unique achievement.

8
TOWNS AND TRADES

A PART from Edinburgh, whose complex townscape requires individual treatment, the Lothians and Borders are not heavily urbanised. Nevertheless, towns have been important as centres of trade and industry from medieval times. It could, indeed, be claimed that the Iron Age tribal capitals of Traprain Law and Eildon Hill North were embryo towns. However, urban life proper did not begin until the twelfth century. Throughout the medieval period, and indeed for centuries after, towns remained small, tight-knit communities with a few basic industries, local market centres closely tied to the surrounding countryside. Many ancient towns – Lauder is a good example – have retained this character into modern times. From the eighteenth century, however, the growth of a range of industries led to many towns developing on a larger scale.

MEDIEVAL BURGHS: FOUNDATION, GROWTH AND FAILURE

An innovation which the Anglophile David I introduced to Scotland, along with feudalism and the monastic orders, was the idea of the burgh as a planned and privileged trading centre. Most early towns were royal burghs, established by the crown, often growing in the shelter of a royal castle which, by the end of the twelfth century, had become the administrative centre of a sheriffdom. The castles at Roxburgh, Selkirk, Jedburgh and Peebles all formed foci for the development of adjacent burghs. An early castle or royal residence may also have existed at Linlithgow while at Haddington, although there is no record of a castle, there was a palace in which Alexander II is supposed to have been born.

Although the new burghs were established on greenfield sites they were often adjacent to pre-existing centres, traces of which still survive in the modern townscape. Peebles provides the best example. The motte of the royal castle was built on a promontory at the junction of the Tweed and the Eddleston Water. The principal street of the royal burgh ran eastwards from the castle gate down this neck of land and still forms the focus of the town. To the west across the Eddleston Water, however, is an area referred to as Old Town from at least the fifteenth century. The medieval parish church of St Andrew, built in the twelfth century and antedating the royal burgh, is located here as is the later Cross Kirk on a site with early-Christian traditions. This seems to have been the original settlement, one which for centuries maintained an identity separate from the royal burgh.

There also seem to have been two communities at Selkirk, but here the older one beside the Ettrick was entirely supplanted by the new foundation on the valley side adjacent to the royal castle. At Jedburgh there were two settlements, both called 'Gedwearde' in the ninth century. Only one developed into the later burgh; where was the other? The place name 'Old Jedburgh' 6.5km (4 miles) up the valley might provide a clue but the name does not seem to have any great antiquity and there is nothing about the site to suggest an early origin. More convincing is the area of Bongate on the opposite side of the Jed Water from the present town centre but barely ½km from the market place. The existence of an early cross here and other archaeological finds suggest that this was the other ancient settlement and the name 'Bongate', the street of the bondmen, may indicate that it continued to exist as a kind of dependent settlement in later times.

Plate 45 This church, with its prominent crown spire, occupies the site of the former royal castle of Peebles which controlled the crossing of the Tweed by a timber bridge (the predecessor of the present stone one)

Fig 20 Burghs in south-east Scotland

   The existence of these dual sites indicates that the early history of many burghs was far from simple. Even after they had been established the layout and site of burghs could change with the varying fortunes of accident, trade and war. This can be seen in the complex of sites west of Kelso. Superficially the location of the town can be explained simply: it grew around the medieval abbey at a suitable ford, and later bridging point, on the Tweed, deriving protection from the nearby royal castle of Roxburgh. However, north-east of the castle on the river flats in the angle between the Tweed and Teviot is the site of the lost burgh of Roxburgh. At one time Roxburgh was one of Scotland's major burghs, prospering as a centre for the wool trade beside the first bridge over the Tweed above Berwick.

Surviving charters indicate that by the mid-twelfth century a new planned burgh had been added to the original nucleus close to the castle, the two settlements growing into a single unit. By the

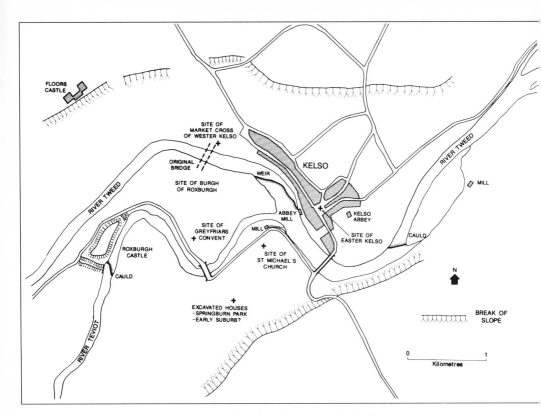

Fig 21 Urban development in the Kelso area

thirteenth century the extended burgh was a walled town with stone churches. In the early fourteenth century the inhabitants swore fealty to Edward I who gave them permission to raise money to replace their earth and timber defences with a stone wall. However, Roxburgh was too close to the Border for comfort. Together with the adjacent castle it was alternatively in English and Scottish hands throughout the fourteenth and fifteenth centuries. When it was finally recaptured by the Scots in 1460 the town was already in decay. In 1545 the Earl of Hertford drew up a list of all the settlements in the area that he had burnt: Roxburgh was omitted. There was nothing left to destroy on the site of the once proud town.

The monks of Kelso Abbey took advantage of the growth of trade generated by Roxburgh in its heyday by having a burgh of their own established in the thirteenth century. The site of this settlement, Wester Kelso, in the grounds of Floors Castle where the old road from Edinburgh ran down to the Tweed, has recently been located by excavation. The later history of the site is unclear. One suggestion is that it had declined by the fifteenth century in favour of the settlement around the abbey a short distance downstream. Another

160

possibility is that it was Wester Kelso rather than the modern Kelso that was devastated by fire in 1684 and that it was never rebuilt. The old mercat cross of Wester Kelso continued to stand on the site of the former burgh into the late-eighteenth century and annual cattle fairs were still held around it, the last vestige of the trading privileges of the vanished settlement. South of the Teviot, in Springwood Park, recent excavations have also uncovered traces of Roxburgh's early suburb (720334). The foundations of three stone houses aligned parallel to the river terrace were superimposed on those of two earlier buildings laid out at right angles. Indications were that the site had been abandoned in the late-thirteenth century. The history of urban development in this interesting area is thus a complex one.

MEDIEVAL BURGHS: FORM AND FABRIC

The layout of many burghs followed a standard pattern with a single main street widening in the centre or at one end to form a market place. In Lauder you can see the two back lanes which ran parallel to the market place giving access to the rear of the building plots. At Peebles the royal castle formed the anchor point from which the burgh was laid out, the wide main street running straight from the castle gate. The castle appears to have lost its strategic significance after the Wars of Independence and was abandoned by the mid-fourteenth century. At Jedburgh the royal castle also dominated the main street although in conjunction with the abbey. It was demolished in the early-fifteenth century and the site is now occupied by an early-nineteenth century jail. At Hawick the castle motte is placed on the edge of the town as though it was a peripheral addition to an existing settlement. Similar single-street plans are also found in Linlithgow, Lauder and Haddington although Selkirk has a series of roads converging on a central market place. From either side of the main street of these early burghs, lines of building plots or 'burgages' ran back at right angles forming a herringbone pattern. Each burgess in the medieval town was granted one of these plots and was expected to reside on it and establish himself in trade or manufacturing. This straightforward layout is the basis of the plans of most burghs in the Lothians and the Borders, including Edinburgh. It is best appreciated, on the map or on the ground, in a small town like Lauder.

Some market places have been 'colonised' by islands of building which sometimes contain the town house or tolbooth. This can be seen at Lauder and in a more complicated manner at Haddington. Haddington's medieval market place, a long triangular area with its

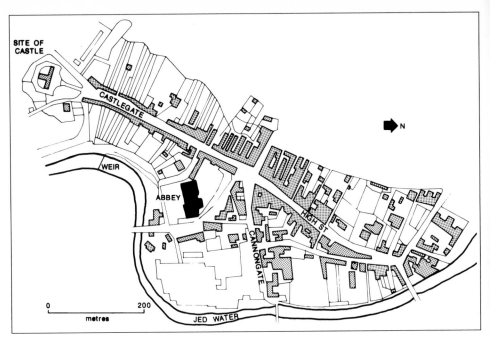

Fig 22 The medieval layout of Jedburgh

apex pointing west and its base on the cross-streets of Hardgate and Sidegate, must have been one of noble dimensions but it has been chopped up into a number of streets, some of them still quite wide, with islands of building in between.

The symbolic expression in stone of a burgh's right to trade was its mercat cross around which merchants gathered to conduct business and from which proclamations were read. Originally set up on a stone base in the centre of the market place many crosses have been resited or removed due to the demands of modern traffic. The one at Dunbar stands beside the tolbooth while Haddington's, fairly recent but last in a long line, also stands in an inconspicuous position. In addition Haddington has the medieval custom stone at the junction of the High Street and Hardgate where market tolls were paid. One of the oldest surviving mercat crosses stands at the east end of the main street of Peebles, on a site close to its original location. The shaft and the carved capital that surmounts it date from the fifteenth century. The carvings, though weathered, show the arms of the burgh and those of the Frasers of Oliver and Neidpath, a local family who were once influential in the town as hereditary sheriffs. The fact that the family had declined by the early-

Plate 46 The old tolbooth of Dunbar, built around 1620, served as a council chamber and prison. The old mercat cross of Dunbar stands beside it

fourteenth century suggests that the existing cross may have been copied from an earlier one.

The principal civic building of these burghs was the tolbooth, a structure which served as courthouse, prison and place for collecting market dues. Musselburgh has the finest, dating from around 1590 though its tower may be earlier. It has a fortress-like appearance and clearly derives many of its features from contemporary tower houses. Like a tower house the building is stone vaulted and there is no internal communication between the ground floor and the first floor which is reached by an external forestair. Dunbar's tolbooth, dating from around 1620, is dominated by a five-sided stair tower rising to a steeple. In Haddington the old tolbooth has been replaced by a more stylish classical town house designed by William Adam in 1752.

Few medieval Scottish burghs were walled but because of the threat from across the Border as well as from local bands of reivers, several towns in south-east Scotland possessed defences. The early burghs of Roxburgh and Berwick were defended by earthworks and timber palisades which were replaced during the fourteenth century by stone defensive walls. The cost of building and maintaining such a wall was considerable and few towns could afford such a luxury. Because of this it is curious that the burgesses of Peebles, a small town with no real strategic significance, decided to have a stone wall strengthened with towers built around the town. Even more remarkably this was done as late as the 1570s when Border warfare was declining. The Regent Moray, visiting Peebles in 1569, urged the provost and baillies to build the wall to resist attacks by thieves from the Scottish side of the Border. In 1571, while the wall was under construction, a band of raiders – Armstrongs, Elliots, Grahams, and Johnstones, Scotsmen all – broke into the town and plundered a number of houses. The wall was maintained into the early-eighteenth century but was then allowed to decay. Sections of it can still be seen on the east side of Northgate, the road leading towards Edinburgh, along with a tower containing two gunports.

In other towns the wall was less a defensive work than a boundary to mark the limits of the burgh, restrict the entry of undesirables and prevent people from sneaking in without paying market tolls. Traffic was channelled through gateways or 'ports' barring the main streets which served as toll barriers and for regulating who was admitted to the town. None of these gateways have survived but their former existence, preserved in street names and plaques, does not necessarily imply that they were accompanied by substantial walls. Haddington had one of these modest walls, running along the bottom of the

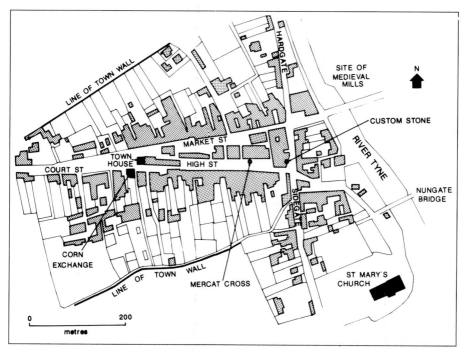

Fig 23 The medieval layout of Haddington

burgage plots, traces of which can still be seen (515742). Known as the 'King's Wall' it dates from the fifteenth century. On the south of the town its line is clearly marked by a lane called the Butts. Haddington's 'ports' were demolished long since to allow traffic to move more easily. Dunbar too had its wall. A late-sixteenth century visitor described the town as 'fenced in by a stone wall of great strength'. This may have been an exaggeration because there is nothing in the fabric of the town today to suggest massive defences. The town's three ports were, like the West Port in Haddington, demolished in the later-eighteenth century but the line of Dunbar's wall is still marked by a lane running along the bottom of the burgage plots.

Originally only the heads of the burgage plots fronting on to the main street were built up. The tails of the plots were left open as gardens and smallholdings. As the population grew and pressure on space increased the plots were infilled with additional housing and workshops at right angles to the main street, reached by access ways or 'closes' leading through the buildings facing on to the market place. This infilling is well seen in Haddington in examples like the attractively-restored Mitchell's Close where one- and two-storey workshops run back behind the three- and four-storey houses facing the main street.

165

While the street plans and layout of the building plots often go back to medieval times the houses which stand on them are generally much later in date. Most towns have a Georgian or Victorian appearance modified by later additions, with little predating the later-eighteenth century. Sometimes a walk round to the backs of the buildings will show that they are actually older, perhaps from the seventeenth century, and have been re-fronted. Unaltered seventeenth-century houses are not common; earlier dwellings are even rarer. Until well into the seventeenth century most houses were timber-framed with thatched roofs. They were replaced by stone walled, slate roofed houses during later, more prosperous times. In Peebles many such houses survived into the nineteenth century and the last were not removed until the 1870s. Alternatively, houses of this type were removed by fire, by enemy action as during the English invasions of the 1540s, or by accident. A large section of Peebles was destroyed in this way in 1704 while most of Kelso was reduced to ashes in 1684.

BURGHS OF BARONY

During the sixteenth and seventeenth centuries a number of new burghs of barony were created in addition to existing royal burghs and older baronial foundations like Dalkeith, Duns, Hawick, Kelso and Musselburgh. Until the later-seventeenth century burghs of barony were not supposed to engage in foreign trade and had only restricted rights to internal trade. Accordingly, most of them remained small, mere villages whose markets and fairs served only a scatter of surrounding *ferm touns*.

Some royal burghs also remained small, like South Queensferry and Lauder, but nevertheless took their status seriously having a merchant guild and a range of craft incorporations. Almost all, even the smallest, carried on some overseas trade. Several royal burghs were disadvantaged in this respect because of their inland location. Border burghs like Jedburgh had an active overland trade with England whenever political conditions permitted. Haddington and Linlithgow overcame the problems of their location by having official ports, Aberlady and Blackness respectively, through which their merchants could operate.

Agriculture was a part-time activity for most burgesses. Each town had its burgh fields in which the burgesses had shares. They also had areas of common pasture on which the burgh's herds and flocks could graze under the watchful eye of the herdsman. These common pastures were sometimes extensive: Dunbar had a large area in the

Lammermuirs which it sold off in the nineteenth century to finance the construction of the Victoria Harbour.

At Lauder the town lands remained intact into the twentieth century. Lauder had 105 'burgess acres', occupation of which continued to give the owners the qualification of 'burgess'. Owners of burgess acres had a fixed share in the common pasture. Perambulating the boundaries of their commons to check on possible encroachments by neighbouring landowners was a regular necessity. Peebles, for instance, had in the sixteenth century a series of disputes with local proprietors over grazing rights which led to violence and bloodshed on more than one occasion. Riding the bounds of a burgh's common land became ritualised into a kind of civic pageant, a celebration of each town's independence, in which history and tradition were merged. These survive today as the Common Ridings of the Border towns. At Hawick the ceremony commemorates the success of the burgh's inhabitants in driving off an English raiding force in 1514 and capturing their colours. At Selkirk it is the tragic defeat at Flodden which is remembered. Supposedly only a single survivor returned of the men who left to fight for James IV and today a lone horseman casts his colours down in the market place to keep the memory alive.

THE BORDER MILL TOWNS AND THE WOOLLEN INDUSTRY

One of the most distinctive industries in south-east Scotland is the Border woollen industry. Although the medieval monastic houses raised huge flocks of sheep on the Border hills the development of woollen manufacture only occurred from the late-eighteenth century. Before this woollen yarn had been spun in almost every Border household and had been made up into coarse cloth by local weavers but production was small scale and largely for the domestic market. The wool of the local Blackface sheep was coarse and was virtually ruined for making all but the poorest fabrics by the practice of smearing sheep with tar mixed with other substances including butter and, from the seventeenth century, tobacco juice. This was supposed to protect the sheep from the weather, and also from disease, but it was hardly conducive to improving the wool!

Efforts were made in the later-seventeenth century to establish manufactories which would produce higher-quality cloth. One at New Mills outside Haddington and others at Musselburgh and in Berwickshire operated for a few years and employed large numbers of outworkers. The cloth that they manufactured was always more expensive than English cloth of similar quality. After the Union of

Plate 47 Paties' Mill, Carlops. A small water-powered carding mill which was associated with weavers' cottages. It later became a grain mill and is now a private house

1707, the manufactories were opened to the full effects of English competition and rapidly went out of business.

The manufacture of woollens in the Borders grew only slowly during the eighteenth century. The most important change which underlay the development of the industry was the spread of the Cheviot sheep whose wool was of higher quality than the Blackface and whose fleece was no longer tarred. This provided a local supply of better-quality wool and gradually industry began to respond. Although there was local wool and abundant water power the Borders were remote from other industrial areas and transport costs were high.

In the later-eighteenth century the Border textile industries were still small-scale and scattered. Many rural workers wove cloth part-time in the slack periods of the farming year. A number of planned villages were set up with the aim of encouraging weaving. Newcastleton in Liddesdale was the largest while Carlops, south of Edinburgh, was developed on a more modest scale. Even when the industry began to go over to factory production the scale of activity was still small. At Denholm near Hawick you can still see two early stocking-weaving factories. One is a three-storey building but still a modest construction compared with the scale of mills a century later.

The first efforts at mechanising the woollen industry occurred at

Innerleithen. Here, in 1788, a four-storey yarn spinning mill was set up by Alexander Brodie, a local blacksmith who had made a fortune in the Shropshire iron trade. The mill, only slightly altered, can still be seen (332370) but although it was a local wonder in its day it was never profitable in Brodie's lifetime. The mechanised woollen industry concentrated in two places, Galashiels and Hawick. Galashiels was a mere village in the 1780s, whose development was vigorously promoted by the local landowning family, the Scotts of Gala, who released plots of land to industrialists. The first water-powered mills were built there in 1791 and half a dozen more followed in the next few years; soon Galashiels was growing rapidly. Hawick, an established town with medieval origins, developed in the later eighteenth century as a centre for framework knitting, particularly of woollen hose and underwear. Outlying woollen centres included Jedburgh, Melrose and Peebles. Both the Gala Water and River Teviot, on which the two major centres stood, had a steep gradient allowing water-powered mills to be clustered in groups. Both towns grew up in constricted valley-bottom sites without any coherent planning; rows of workers' cottages and mills are intermingled. In Selkirk the woollen industry developed from the 1850s as an overspill from nearby Galashiels. Here there was a sharper separation between the medieval burgh on the slope above the Ettrick Water and the new mills on the flat haugh lands beside the river.

In the 1820s much of the cloth produced in this area was still of fairly low quality. The origins of Border tweeds lay in the black and white checked plaids which were produced for local shepherds, using the natural colour of the local wool. Tourists and visitors began to discover the warmth-generating, hard-wearing qualities of this cloth. At the same time interest in tartans was developing with the popularity of the works of Sir Walter Scott. Scott himself actively promoted Border woollens among fashionable circles. The shepherd's check became popular as a material for trousers as well as plaids and was soon fashionable in London. In the mid 1830s a clerk of a London clothier misread the name 'tweel' (the Scottish version of 'twill', the term for this particular type of material) as 'tweed'. This happy accident gave rise to a product name that became world famous.

Even in its early phases of development when water was the principal source of power the industries of Galashiels and Hawick needed some coal. It was brought laboriously and expensively by road, over distances of 32–48km (20–30 miles). The coming of the railways in the 1850s greatly cheapened the price of coal and allowed many mills to go over to steam power, though water power remained important throughout the nineteenth century. A new generation of mills, built during the second half of the nineteenth century and in many cases still in use, reflect the growing prosperity of the industry. They are bigger, with larger windows providing more light than the earlier ones, and they still dominate the townscapes of Galashiels, Hawick and Selkirk. Mechanisation of weaving came later than the application of power to spinning. This was partly due to technical difficulties with the weaving of high-quality cloth. Although some power looms were in operation in the 1830s they were not widely used until the 1860s. The handloom weaver working in his own cottage gradually gave way to the factory employee operating a power loom. Large single-storey weaving sheds were built alongside the taller spinning mills.

The industry spread up the Tweed to Peebles, where three mills were built from the 1850s. Other outlying mill communities remained fairly small. The fall of water on the Tweed was so gentle that mills could not be as tightly grouped as on the faster-flowing tributaries Teviot and Gala Water. At Innerleithen, Ballantyne and Co. took over Alexander Brodie's late-eighteenth century mill. In the 1840s three more mills were built as the industry expanded. St Ronan's Mill, on the northern outskirts of the town, is a fine example of mid-nineteenth century mill construction. Three storeys in height, with a double line of attic windows in the roof, it is still used for spinning yarn and is designed in a style which still reflects local influences rather than those of industrial England, as the later-nineteenth century mills were to do. Ballantyne and Co. also developed Walkerburn, between Innerleithen and Galashiels, as a textile-making village. One of the mills there now houses the Scottish Museum of Woollen Textiles.

Mining, Salt Making and Quarrying

Another distinctive group of towns developed along the shores of the Lothians in the seventeenth century based on coal mining and salt making. Foremost were Prestonpans and Bo'ness. Bo'ness was one of the fastest growing towns in Scotland in the later-seventeenth century as a result of these industries and the spin-off into shipping and other activities. Coal was mined along the coast adjacent to these centres and the better quality lumps were exported. The dross or 'small coal' was put to profitable use as fuel for producing salt by evaporating sea water in large shallow iron pans. At one time during the seventeenth century Scottish salt, much of it produced around the Firth of Forth, was one of the country's major exports.

Despite competition from purer Cheshire rock salt the industry survived in a small way until as late as 1958 in Prestonpans and the building which housed the last Scottish saltworks can still be seen. The availability of a cheap fuel supply attracted other industries to the Prestonpans area, notably pottery. In the eighteenth century there were a number of pottery works along the coast between Musselburgh and Seton. Although few traces of the buildings associated with them have survived, shards of pottery can be found around the sites as can pieces of imported flint which were used in making the glaze and which did not occur locally. Further west, at Portobello, two large bottle kilns, built in the early twentieth century, survive from the pottery there.

Before the nineteenth century coal was mined mainly where seams outcropped along the coast or lay close to the surface. Coal mining went back to medieval times and the monks of Newbattle Abbey are among the earliest recorded miners in the Lothians. As late as the eighteenth century much of the coal was obtained by digging primitive 'bell pits' to reach shallow seams. Shafts were sunk and the coal was cut away in all directions from the base of the shaft, producing a bell-shaped section, until drainage difficulties developed or roof-falls threatened, whereupon the workings were abandoned and a new bell pit was sunk. In most coalfield areas these primitive workings have been obliterated by later large-scale mining but they can still be seen at one or two localities where they tapped seams which were too thin to be considered profitable in later times. Some shallow medieval workings have been preserved at Birsley Brae to the west of Tranent and bell pits can also be seen near Carlops where the modern opencast workings exploit the same shallow seams.

As the industry grew in scale during the nineteenth century so did the size of individual pits. Remains of many of the larger collieries are still prominent although their spoil heaps have often been removed or landscaped. The history of coal mining in the Lothians is well displayed at two collieries which have been preserved. One at Prestongrange, east of Musselburgh, houses the Scottish Mining Museum. Coal was worked here from medieval times but the colliery whose remains can be seen today was first opened in 1830. The centrepiece of the museum is a huge beam engine installed in 1874 for pumping water from the workings. It is housed in a tall, narrow engine house close to which are a line of Hoffman kilns from a brick and fireclay works. A range of other mining equipment from neighbouring collieries has been collected here including colliery railway engines.

The other mine is the Lady Victoria Colliery at Newtongrange, south of Dalkeith. This mine was developed at the end of the nineteenth century and was closed in 1981. Most of the surface buildings have been preserved including the pithead gear and steam winding engine, the largest in Scotland. They give a good impression of what a colliery was like in the heyday of mining. Adjacent is the village of Newtongrange, built by the coal company and the largest pit-village in Scotland. The terraced houses were built with small front gardens for flowers and larger vegetable gardens behind. They are laid out on a grid plan whose streets are rather unimaginatively called First Street, Second Street and so on. The company also provided a miners' institution, recreation ground and bowling green for its workers. In this part of Midlothian you can find other pit villages although the worst of the colliery housing has been demolished. Rosewell is the most complete example, built with a distinctive yellowish brick which looks very alien to Scotland.

The most distinctive mining industry in the Lothians, due to the huge quantities of waste which were produced, was oil shale extraction. The discovery that oil could be distilled from the shale deposits of West Lothian was made by James 'Paraffin' Young in 1850. The industry grew rapidly and by 1865 there were some 120 works in operation. Output peaked early in the present century and competition from oil produced more cheaply from Texas and elsewhere caused a decline in production, though the last works did not close until the 1960s. Despite this the legacy of the oil shale industry in the landscape is still evident in the huge reddish spoil heaps or 'bings'. The bings are flat topped in contrast to the conical ones produced from coal mining. The vast amounts of waste material produced by the industry made large flat spoil heaps much more economical. Many have been removed in recent years for use in road making. Those that remain may be considered an eyesore but there is no denying their visual impact. The industry also gave rise to a number of new settlements including Broxburn, Dalmeny, Pump-herston and Winchburgh whose single-storey brick cottages, like their counterparts in some of the mining villages, have a distinctly un-Scottish appearance.

An industry which, for geological reasons, was concentrated in the Lothians and northern Peebles-shire was the quarrying and burning of lime. Lime was used in the manufacture of mortar and also as an agricultural fertiliser. Its properties for reducing soil acidity and improving crop yields were first discovered by farmers in the Lothians in the early seventeenth century. As time went on the level of demand increased and the technology of lime burning improved.

Plate 48 Old lime kilns at Whitfield near West Linton, an important lime-producing area in the eighteenth and nineteenth centuries

Early lime kilns were crude clamp kilns made largely of turf, which had to be broken open when each load of lime had been burnt. Examples can still be seen at Whitfield near Carlops (169530). A later improvement was the draw kiln, built of stone (often with a heat-resistant brick lining) and usually constructed against a slope so that cartloads of fuel and limestone could be dropped in from the top and the lime removed at the base in a continuous process.

Many of these kilns can still be seen. There is a good example, with an explanatory board, on the coast at Catcraig south of Dunbar, in the shadow of a large modern cement works, and at Skateraw, further down the coast, where a harbour was constructed for shipping out the burnt lime. Skateraw also supplied large quantities of lime to farmers in the Merse. Farmers brought their carts many miles to Skateraw where there were sometimes queues of over a hundred at a time waiting to be loaded before making the long journey home fully laden. In Midlothian the quarries and kilns around Middleton formed a huge complex with a quarry face 0.8km (0.5 mile) long. In some parts of the Lothians the Carboniferous limestones are so thinly bedded that they have been worked by mining rather than quarrying. Limestone mines can be seen at Bowdenhill and Hillhouse south of Linlithgow and at Burdiehouse south of Edinburgh. The limestone was extracted by the simple 'pillar and stall' technique whereby pillars of unquarried rock were left to support the roof. The mines often descended at a steep angle, following the bedding planes of the limestone, and drainage by means of pumping equipment or adit levels was required.

9

THE MAKING
OF EDINBURGH:
THE OLD TOWN

HILLS AND LAKES: EDINBURGH'S DISTINCTIVE SITE

EDINBURGH'S distinctive site is familiar from innumerable photographs and descriptions. Nevertheless, it has so strongly influenced the growth of the city, and controlled the layout of its streets and buildings, that it is worth emphasising its basic features here. There are a number of good vantage points from which you can appreciate Edinburgh's topography; the top of Salisbury Crags, the battlements of the Castle or the summit of Calton Hill are among the best. From any of these summits you can see how irregular the topography of the area is. The rock on which the Castle stands is only one of a number of volcanic hills which break up the coastal plain of the Lothians where it narrows between the Pentlands and the Firth of Forth. The eroded volcano of Arthur's Seat, and the imposing rampart of Salisbury Crags are the highest and most dramatic of them. These steep hills attracted prehistoric settlers and you can trace the remains of a rampart round the summit of Arthur's Seat. The lower summits include Blackford Hill, the Braid Hills, Calton Hill, Corstorphine Hill, and the Castle Rock. The last of these formed the nucleus from which the city was to grow.

The Castle Rock was the most defensible of the lower hills with precipitous cliffs on all sides except the east. The rock and the long, steep-sided ridge descending eastwards from it are a classic glacial 'crag and tail'. Ice sheets moving eastwards from the Highlands plucked and abraded the Castle Rock into an almost unscalable cliff. Moving around the obstruction the ice scoured deep hollows on either side of the rock which are now occupied by Princes Street Gardens on the north and the Cowgate on the south. In the lee of the crag, however, a tail of softer sedimentary rocks was protected

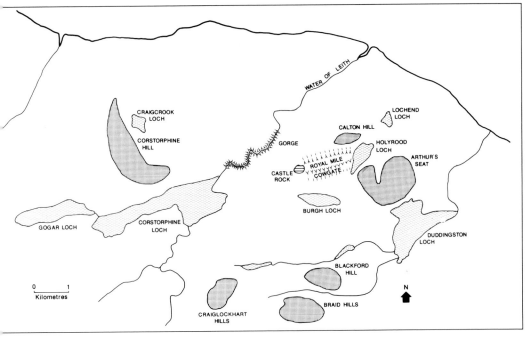

Fig 24 The site of Edinburgh

from erosion. This tail forms the ridge down the crest of which the Royal Mile descends gradually from the Castle to Holyrood Palace.

Edinburgh's hills are still dramatic and obvious to the modern visitor. Between them, however, there was once a series of lakes and marshes which also helped to create a secure site for the city and influenced the directions in which it grew. Only a few remnants of these lakes now exist, including Duddingston, Dunsapie and Loch-end Lochs, but formerly they were more numerous and more extensive. Some survived into comparatively recent times. The city was still using the Burgh Loch (now drained to form the area of parkland known as the Meadows) for part of its water supply as late as the sixteenth century. The reclamation of the largest lake, Corstorphine Loch, was only completed in 1837.

Another important feature of Edinburgh's site was its lack of a river. The provision of an adequate water supply and the removal of waste was made difficult as a result. Combined with the high density of building this lack of a natural sewage-disposal system helped to give the city a reputation for dirty streets and foul smells. Edinburgh was something of a rarity: a pre-industrial capital city without immediate access to navigable water. The shallow Water of Leith, which flowed to the west of the Old Town, was large enough to drive a string of water mills but was useless for navigation. Edinburgh's need for an outlet on the Firth of Forth led to the early establishment of the port of Leith and the later development of other harbours like Newhaven and Granton.

The deep-cut valleys on either side of the ridge which descended eastwards from the Castle restricted Edinburgh's growth to the end of the eighteenth century. This was particularly the case to the north where the marshy valley was dammed to form the Nor Loch, a source of water for the medieval town and a dumping place for refuse. The land beyond, where Princes Street and the New Town now stand, remained open country until the later-eighteenth century. To the south, the city spread across the deep but drier divide of the Cowgate by the end of the fifteenth century. However, access to the city from this direction involved either a steep direct climb or a long detour eastwards via the Canongate. On the more level ground on the far side of the Cowgate the city's first suburbs were built. The constricted nature of Edinburgh's site controlled its street plan. It also helped to make the Old Town the most tightly-packed city in Europe with a unique concentration of high-rise buildings.

Fig 25 View of Edinburgh in 1650, showing the profile of the crag and tail landform on which the castle and the medieval town were built

THE ORIGINS AND GROWTH OF THE MEDIEVAL CITY

Edinburgh's origins are closely linked with the fortress on the Castle Rock in whose shelter the medieval town developed. It is uncertain whether there was a fort here in prehistoric times as later building activities have obliterated the earliest traces of occupation. However, considering its defensive qualities such a use of the site is likely. The survival and continued development of the Castle Rock marked it out from other early defensive sites in the Lothians. For example, the Dark-Age fortress on Traprain Law, a major tribal capital before and during the Roman occupation, was abandoned during the seventh century AD.

Historical records suggest that in the centuries after the withdrawal of the Romans from Britain the fortress on the Castle Rock was the capital of the Gododdin, a people whose territory coincided broadly with the later Lothians. Their citadel was called Din Eidyn in Brythonic and later Dun Eideann in Gaelic. The kingdom of Gododdin came under pressure from the expanding Anglian kingdom of Bernicia, whose forces captured Din Eidyn in 636 AD. The conquerers adapted the name to their own language and called it 'Edinburgh'. The Anglian hold over Edinburgh and the country around it was fairly brief. The Lothians were re-absorbed into the expanding Scottish kingdom during the ninth and tenth centuries. With political stability and the pushing of the frontier with England well to the south the scene was set for the development of the first proper town on this site.

There is likely to have been a settlement of some kind outside the gates of the fortress on the Castle Rock from Dark Age times at least. However, the first real town was a planned venture by the Scottish king David I. Edinburgh, founded around 1124, was one of his new burghs, established on the Anglo-Norman model as described in Chapter 8. Although one of Scotland's first burghs, Edinburgh did not develop immediately as the capital. In early medieval times the heart of the Scottish kingdom lay further north around the Firth of Tay and the castle at Edinburgh was just one of many royal centres occupied by peripatetic monarchs. During the Wars of Independence in the early-fourteenth century Edinburgh was too close to the Border and too vulnerable to be a safe capital. It was not until the fifteenth century that Edinburgh was formally declared to be the capital and permanent seat of government.

Like most medieval towns Edinburgh was small. David I's royal burgh only extended from the gates of the castle halfway down the crest of the ridge to the east. In 1385 the French chronicler Froissart

177

wrote that the town contained fewer than 400 houses. From the sixteenth century, however, Scotland's urban population increased at a rate which was among the fastest in Europe: nearly twice that of England. Edinburgh, although remaining small in area, rapidly became a substantial city in terms of population. During the sixteenth and seventeenth centuries Edinburgh was comparable in size with, or rather bigger than, Norwich, England's largest provincial centre. While Edinburgh could not compete with giants like London, Paris or Amsterdam the burgh was equivalent in size to many second-rank continental cities. Its size, and particularly the density of its buildings, certainly impressed many English and overseas visitors. Edinburgh's population in the mid-sixteenth century was probably between 9,000 and 15,000, depending on whether one includes the suburbs and the port of Leith. The population is thought to have doubled between the mid-sixteenth and mid-seventeenth centuries, the bulk of it still accommodated within the 57ha (140 acres) of the royal burgh itself. By the early eighteenth century the city, including its satellites, may have held up to 50,000 inhabitants. For a country with a population of little more than a million at the opening of the eighteenth century, whose economy was backward and impoverished compared with most of her neighbours, the creation of a city the size of Edinburgh was no mean achievement.

THE LAYOUT OF THE OLD TOWN

Edinburgh's development outside the gates of a royal castle can be paralleled in other Scottish burghs. However, the nature of Edinburgh's site played an important part in determining the layout of the city. Given that proximity to the Castle was desirable for protection, the most logical plan for the town was one with the main axis oriented down the crest of the gently-sloping tail to the east of the Castle Rock. This had the additional advantage of providing a defensive position of some strength. The street which ran from the Castle to Holyrood Palace had become known by the sixteenth century as the Royal Mile. It was probably laid out on the line of an older track leading from the Castle Rock to another ancient route crossing the ridge roughly where the later boundary between Edinburgh and the Canongate was drawn.

Edinburgh's street plan is a conventional medieval one found elsewhere in Scotland and throughout Europe. A single straight thoroughfare widens in the centre to form a market place. On either side of the street building plots or burgages ran back at right angles in long strips from narrow frontages. The street plan of the medieval town has remained its most enduring feature, followed by the building plots, many of which are fossilised in modern property boundaries. The medieval buildings, apart from the Castle, St Giles and Holyrood Abbey, were relatively flimsy and have not survived at all. Nevertheless, the later structures which replaced them were shaped and constrained by the inherited framework of streets and building plots.

In Edinburgh the burgages averaged 7.6m (25ft) in width and 137m (450ft) in length giving each plot an area of one rood, or a quarter of an acre. As in other medieval towns only the street frontages of the plots, the 'forelands', were built up initially. When pressure for more accommodation grew new buildings, the 'back-lands', were constructed towards the rear. This process of infilling was well advanced by the end of the fifteenth century. Access to the backlands was provided by narrow alleyways between or under the forelands. These became known as 'closes' or sometimes 'wynds' and 'vennels'. They were often spaced about 7.6m (25ft) apart reflecting the old property boundaries.

The names of the closes sometimes reflected local landmarks and prominent buildings such as Bakehouse Close and Old Stamp Office Close. Mostly, however, they derived their names from families which occupied the forelands from which they led off. As the names of owners of the forelands changed so did those of the closes, providing later historians with a complex puzzle! For instance Dickson's Close near the Netherbow Port was also known at various times as Bruce's, Haliburton's, Catchpole's, Machan's and Aikman's Close! Wynds were common access ways and were usually through routes, but closes were private, often cul-de-sacs, and could be shut off by gates. Examples of each kind can still be seen on either side of the High Street. An important development, mainly during the seventeenth century, was the amalgamation of many burgages and their re-development into courtyards, surrounded by tenements. These courtyards were located behind the street frontages and sometimes inter-communicated. Wardrop's Court and James' Court on the north side of the Lawnmarket are good examples surrounded by some fine seventeenth-century high-rise housing.

DEFENDING THE CITY

The Castle was the nucleus from which Edinburgh developed and it remained an important focus within the city into modern times. Often besieged, its strong site meant that it was rarely captured by

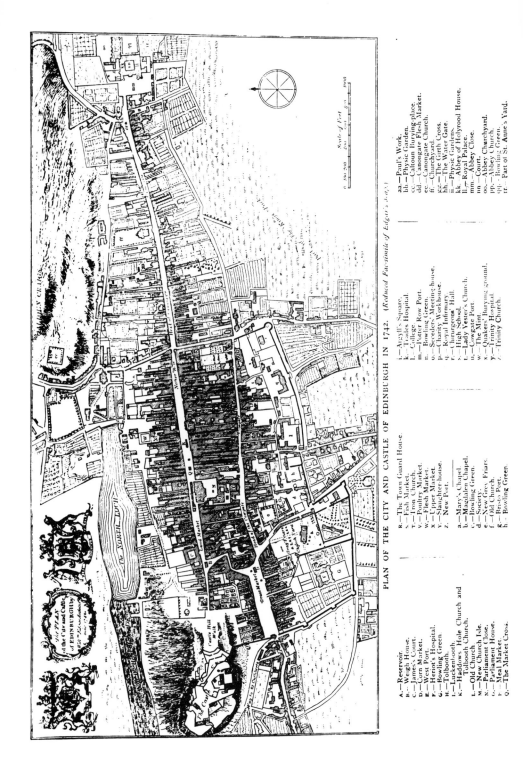

PLAN OF THE CITY AND CASTLE OF EDINBURGH IN 1742. (Reduced Fac-simile of Edgar's Map.)

A.—Reservoir.
B.—Weigh House.
c.—James's Court.
D.—Corn Market.
E.—West Port.
F.—Heriot's Hospital.
G.—Bowling Green.
H.—Tolbooth.
I.—Luckenbooth.
k.—Haddows' Hole Church and Tolbooth Church.
L.—Old Church.
M.—New Church Isle.
N.—Parliament Close.
O.—Parliament House.
P.—Meal Market.
Q.—The Market Cross.

R.—The Town Guard House
S.—Fish Market.
T.—Iron Church.
U.—Poultry Market.
W.—Flesh Market.
X.—Upper Market.
Y.—Slaughter-house.
Z.—New Port.

a.—Mary's Chapel.
b.—Magdalene Chapel.
c.—Society.
d.—New Grey Friars.
e.—Old Church.
f.—Bristo Port.
g.—Bowling Green.
h.—Bowling Green.

i.—Argyll's Square.
k.—Trades Hospital.
l.—College.
m.—Potter Row Port.
n.—Bowling Green.
o.—Screders' Meeting-house.
p.—Charity Workhouse.
q.—Royal Infirmary.
r.—Surgeons' Hall.
s.—Physic Gardens.
t.—Lady Yester's Church.
u.—High School.
v.—Cowgate Port.
w.—The Mint.
x.—Quakers' Burying ground.
y.—Trinity Hospital.
z.—Trinity Church.

aa.—Paul's Work.
bb.—Physic Garden.
cc.—Caltoun Burying-place.
dd.—Canongate Flesh Market.
ee.—Canongate Church.
ff.—Churchyard.
gg.—The Girth Cross.
hh.—The Water Gate.
ii.—Physic Gardens.
kk.—Abbey of Holyrood House.
ll.—Royal Palace.
mm.—Abbey Close.
nn.—Court.
oo.—Abbey Churchyard.
pp.—Abbey Church.
qq.—Bowling Green.
rr.—Part of St. Anne's Yard.

direct assault although its defenders were starved out on more than one occasion. Its last siege occurred during the Jacobite rebellion of 1745. The appearance of the Castle is so familiar that a detailed description of it is unnecessary but a few points about its development should be emphasised. The castle which survives today is a composite structure spanning several centuries. The earliest building is the Norman chapel of St Margaret, thought to have been built for David I in memory of his mother. The more recent additions, including the eighteenth- and nineteenth-century barrack blocks and hospital, dominate the skyline of the Castle, particularly from Princes Street and the west. Until the eighteenth century large areas on the summit of the Castle Rock remained open; defences were concentrated on the eastern side which offered the only easy access.

The destruction caused by various sieges and the need to keep up with changing military technology have resulted in the obliteration or modification of many earlier structures. The Half Moon Battery, the prominent curved bulwark overlooking the Old Town, was built in the 1570s on the ruins of David's Tower, the mid-fourteenth century keep which collapsed under bombardment during the siege of 1573. For most of its history the castle has had a number of functions in addition to that of a fortress. It remained a royal residence until the death of James V in 1542 and has served as a barracks, a prison and an ordnance factory at various periods.

As a royal residence, fortress and garrison the administration of the Castle was separate from that of the city. Even when held by a determined garrison the fortress could only offer Edinburgh limited protection as was shown in 1745 when the Jacobite army captured the city with ease but could make no impression on the Castle. In times of danger the burgesses of the city had to look to their own defence.

Only a few Scottish towns were walled but with Edinburgh the defensible site as well as the town's wealth and strategic importance may have encouraged fortification at an early date. The first references to gates, possibly indicating some kind of defences, come from the late-twelfth century. The earliest defences may have only been a simple palisade, a symbolic delineation of the town's limits rather than a serious attempt at protecting the community. During early medieval times Edinburgh may even have been an open town,

Fig 26 Map of Edinburgh in 1742, showing the high density of building in the royal burgh and the more open character of the Canongate. The line of the Flodden Wall and its later extension around Heriot's Hospital is clearly visible

relying for protection on the marshy ground which surrounded it. The earliest known wall, the King's Wall of c1425–50, ran eastwards from the Castle between the High Street and the Cowgate truncating the burgage plots and enclosing only a limited area. The wall probably marked the limits of building development down the burgages at this time. A section of walling downhill from St Columba's Church in Johnston Terrace below the Castle is the longest surviving fragment of the King's Wall. Like the later Flodden Wall it was in many places a makeshift structure utilising existing house and boundary walls. However, a royal decree of 1473 required the demolition of houses which were built on the wall itself, to make it a more effective line of defence. If the burgages south of the High Street originally extended down to the Cowgate their truncation by this wall, effectively contracting the limits of the town, is hardly likely to have been popular with the burgesses. This may explain why two royal charters were necessary to enforce its construction.

After the disastrous Scottish defeat at Flodden in 1513 work on a new wall began though it took more than half a century to complete. This wall enclosed a much larger area to the south than its predecessors, including the Grassmarket and the area where the Old College of the University now stands. It defined the built-up area of Edinburgh until well into the eighteenth century. Sections of the wall used existing boundaries but despite bastions at the corners it was not a particularly impressive defensive system. During the seventeenth and early-eighteenth centuries it was strengthened by the construction of further artillery emplacements. A square tower, still some 6m (20ft) high, can be seen at the head of the Vennel, near the south-west end of the Grassmarket. Another section of the wall forms the present boundary on the north side of Drummond Street near the Old College of the University. The wall was extended between 1628 and 1636 to take in Heriot's Hospital and part of the growing suburb of Easter Portsburgh.

The main gateways or ports were perhaps most useful in regulating the admission of undesirables such as beggars or possible disease carriers during outbreaks of plague. They have all been demolished but brass plates in the roadway where the High Street joins the Canongate mark the site of the Netherbow Port. This was one of the city's ancient gateways which was rebuilt with an imposing set of towers in the early-seventeenth century. Edinburgh's walls were still intact and defensible at the time of the Jacobite rebellion of 1745, though the authorities only made a half-hearted show of manning them. Following the final defeat of the Jacobites they rapidly went out of use and the Netherbow Port was demolished in 1764.

MERCHANTS AND MARKETS

Although Edinburgh had a wide range of industries the city was primarily a trading and adminstrative centre. The original market place was the High Street itself. Craftsmen who had frontages on it could sell goods from wooden counters which let down from the front of their workshops. A reconstructed example of one of these can be seen at Gladstone's Land in the Lawnmarket. Other traders from the town or the surrounding countryside (the 'landward' area after which the name 'Lawnmarket' supposedly derives), could sell their wares from stalls in the street. The congestion which this caused in a thoroughfare which was narrower than the market places of many smaller burghs was often commented on by contemporaries. It was worsened by the process of market colonisation whereby temporary stalls developed into permanent shops. The upper part of the High Street between St Giles and the Lawnmarket became almost completely blocked by buildings. Part of this blockage was caused by the old tolbooth prison, but there was also an accretion of shops known as the Luckenbooths which reduced the width of the High Street to a narrow lane. The Luckenbooths were only cleared away, along with the tolbooth itself, in 1817.

As the population of the city grew markets for particular types of produce were moved off the main streets and dispersed. They were generally placed down closes whose names, like Fishmarket and Fleshmarket Closes, indicate their former locations. The grain market was moved to the north side of the Cowgate below Parliament House with the fish market close by. The flesh market and its adjacent slaughterhouses were shifted to a peripheral site near the Nor Loch where its smell would be less offensive. Despite this the burgh's mercat cross remained in the High Street adjacent to St Giles. It was the symbolic centre of the trading community: from its base proclamations were read and around it merchants gathered to transact business. The Canongate had its own cross which now stands in the parish churchyard. The incorporation of the Grassmarket into the city in the later-fifteenth century provided valuable additional open space for traders and was used as the place of execution until 1784.

The principal public building in late-medieval Edinburgh was the tolbooth. It was known as the 'Heart of Midlothian' and has been immortalised in Scott's novel of the same name. Its site is marked by a heart-shaped setting of stones beside to St Giles. The Canongate tolbooth still survives, an impressive three-storey building with an adjoining tower, complete with gun loops, dating from the later-

sixteenth century. Many of the trades incorporations of the city owned property which they used for meetings, for housing old and infirm guild members or simply rented out. The building belonging to the incorporation of candlemakers, dating from 1722 and now a pub adjoining the Greyfriars Church, is the best example in the upper town. Its peripheral location is due to the fact that the candlemakers' craft was a dangerous fire risk. The candlemakers were banished to this site after a serious fire in 1654 which started in one of their workshops. The Magdalen Chapel in the Cowgate, originally attached to an almshouse, was later converted as a meeting place for the burgh's hammermen, or metal workers. The Canongate has the misleadingly-named Huntly House which formerly belonged to their separate hammermens' guild.

CHURCHES AND ROYAL RESIDENCES

In common with other cities, a good deal of medieval Edinburgh was owned by the church. Holyrood Abbey, founded in 1128 by David I, defined the city's eastward limits. The remains of the nave of the abbey church, dating mainly from the late-twelfth and thirteenth centuries, adjoin the palace. The walls of the ruined choir have been marked out and inside them can be seen the foundations of the first, much smaller, abbey church of 1128. Edinburgh was never a diocesan centre, apart from a five-year spell during the seventeenth century, and the focus of religious life in the royal burgh was the kirk of St Giles. Until the seventeenth century St Giles was the only church within the royal burgh although from 1578 it was split by internal partitions to accommodate the separate congregations of the four parishes into which the royal burgh was divided. The smoothly-finished exterior, which is a nineteenth-century cladding, belies the church's age. The famous crown spire was completed in 1495 and the earliest parts of the surviving structure date from the twelfth century.

The burial ground of St Giles, built over during the construction of Parliament House, was the city's main one until 1562. At that date the Greyfriars churchyard was established on the lands of the former friary. By the seventeenth century the population of the city had grown to such an extent that additional churches were required. The Greyfriars church built in 1620, and the Tron church dating from

Plate 49 The Canongate tolbooth, dating from the late sixteenth century, reflects contemporary tower-house design down to the shot holes and gun loops

1637, are examples. The burgesses of the Canongate worshipped in the abbey church until 1688. Then the congregation was displaced from the abbey when James VII converted it for the use of the Knights of the Thistle and the present Canongate church was built to accommodate the parishioners.

In the later Middle Ages much of the land south of the Cowgate on the edge of the town was acquired by various mendicant orders, principally the Dominican (Black) friars to the east (1230) and the Franciscan (Grey) friars to the west (1443). Their lands and those of the collegiate church of St Mary's in the Fields (the Kirk o'Field, notorious for its association with the murder of Lord Darnley), lay within the Flodden Wall but were not densely built up. They blocked the growth of the city south of the Cowgate until after the Reformation in 1560 when they began to be built over for secular purposes.

Due to the presence of the court until 1603, and the Scottish Parliament and Privy Council until 1707, Edinburgh developed a large professional class, a strong merchant community and a range of luxury trades. Even after 1707 Edinburgh's continued importance as an administrative, educational, legal and social centre maintained this distinctive occupational profile. Originally these functions had developed to serve the court. The castle remained a royal residence into the sixteenth century but from a much earlier date monarchs had found the guest house of Holyrood Abbey to be more comfortable. During the fifteenth century the guest house was enlarged and in 1501 James IV decided to transform it into a proper palace by having an imposing four-storey tower constructed; it forms the north-western end of the present palace. This and its attendant buildings were burnt by the English in 1544 but the tower was rebuilt and the palace extended around three courtyards to something like its present form. The main façade was remodelled under Cromwell's orders and again for Charles II. The other administrative focus lay behind St Giles where Parliament House and the central Scottish law courts were located. The present façade of Parliament House dates from the nineteenth century, replacing a less regular but in many ways more attractive seventeenth-century frontage.

HOUSING IN THE OLD TOWN

The high-rise tenements which line much of the Royal Mile are one of the most distinctive features of the Old Town. They provide a striking contrast to town centres south of the Border and give Edinburgh the appearance of a continental rather than a British city.

Fig 27 A seventeenth-century bird's eye view of the High Street between St Giles and the Tron. The old Parliament House is on the left behind St Giles. In front of the church the Luckenbooths almost block the High Street. Note the high density of housing, with the arcades and external staircases of houses fronting on to the street

The upper part of the High Street has more in common with older residential districts in cities like Paris or Amsterdam than with English towns. The reasons for this high density of housing, which so strongly impressed visitors to Edinburgh from the sixteenth century onwards, were partly related to the nature of the city's site. The deeply-cut valleys on either side of the medieval town helped to

187

restrict its growth as did its walls. The pattern of landholding around the city was also significant. Originally the royal burgh possessed some arable land in the vicinity of the town. It also owned extensive grazings, the Burgh Muir, which extended south to Blackford Hill and east to Duddingston. Portions of this land were sold off piecemeal during the fifteenth century to raise money. By the following century, when the town's population was growing rapidly, the 'royalty', or area over which the burgh's trading privileges extended, was unusually limited. Friction with neighbouring landowners prevented its expansion until well into the eighteenth century. The result of these influences was a city in which the population density was unusually high and the fire risk from the tremendous concentration of housing correspondingly great.

Most houses in medieval Edinburgh, as in other Scottish burghs, were of timber-frame construction with wattle and daub panels and thatched roofs. While the medieval street plan and the layout of the burgage plots have been lasting features of the city many houses were replaced in stone at an early date. Most of the remainder were removed by fire. Like other pre-industrial cities Edinburgh experienced a number of serious accidental blazes. To this may be added the almost total destruction of the town in 1385 by the army of Richard II and serious damage during the Earl of Hertford's invasion of 1544. One or two examples of timber-framed houses in the Lawnmarket survived into the 1870s, late enough to be photographed, before being demolished as slums.

During the sixteenth and seventeenth centuries increasing wealth and the need to build higher to accommodate a rapidly-growing population encouraged large-scale rebuilding in stone. The English attack of 1544, during which extensive areas of the city, particularly in the Canongate, were burnt, also necessitated large-scale rebuilding. Serious fires in 1674, 1676 and 1700 produced stricter controls over the materials from which new houses could be constructed. The Dean of Guild court, which had jurisdiction over matters relating to amenity and land use, imposed regulations forbidding the use of timber framing and requiring roofs to be slated.

Further up the High Street, under pressure of demand for space with a rapidly growing population, this type of house gave way, during the early-seventeenth century, to higher stone tenements. The Scottish tenement is often associated with Victorian industrial towns

Plate 50 John Knox's house is the best example of a sixteenth-century stone town house with projecting wooden galleries

Plate 51 Mylne's Court, a late seventeenth-century tenement with more style and uniformity than earlier housing in Edinburgh

but its origins go much further back. Apartment-style housing was found in pre-industrial Scottish towns. Tenements were a particular feature of Edinburgh though. The confinement of growth in the sixteenth and seventeenth centuries largely within the limits of the Flodden Wall produced one of the densest concentrations of population in Europe. The only way to accommodate people was to build upwards and the scale of high-rise development in the upper part of the old town by the later-seventeenth century was unrivalled. Some tenements, built into the slope dropping down to the Cowgate behind St Giles, had six or seven storeys fronting on to the High Street and as many below facing to the south. Most of these buildings were destroyed in a fire early in the eighteenth century but if you stand near St Giles and look up the High Street to where Lawnmarket narrows between high canyon walls of tenements with the battlements of the Castle towering above, you get an impression of how the town must have looked in the seventeenth century.

An example of an early seventeenth-century tenement survives as

Gladstone's Land in the Lawnmarket. The property was built by Thomas Gledstanes, a merchant, in about 1620. The stone façade may have replaced earlier galleries like those of John Knox's House. Removing projecting timber galleries and building an arcaded stone front in their place allowed Gledstanes to make a permanent encroachment into the street at ground floor level. Nibbling away at the street by extending frontages in this way was a common practice. The medieval High Street was probably wider than it is today but rebuilding in stone from the later sixteenth century was used as an excuse to push the frontages on either side of the street forward by some 6m (20ft). Formerly much of the High Street was arcaded in this fashion. Gladstone's Land is the only original example left although modern ones have been constructed in the Canongate to maintain the tradition. Behind the arcade were two shops. An external forestair on one side gave access to the first floor from which an internal turnpike stair ran to the floors above. A similar forestair can be seen on Moubray House, another seventeenth-century tenement, next to John Knox's House. These external staircases were once common and were often placed less elegantly in the middle of a frontage, cutting off light to the ground floor shops behind. In the 1630s Gladstone's Land accommodated two merchant and three other families. Edinburgh tenements often housed families of markedly contrasting wealth and status; well-to-do occupants tended to live on the lower floors with easier access to the street, poorer families in the attics.

There was little scope for redevelopment in central Edinburgh unless in the wake of major fires. After the blaze of 1674 a good deal of new building was encouraged by the burgh council's exemption of new stone-fronted houses, which replaced timber ones, from taxes for 17 years. By the late-seventeenth century the cramped conditions of many tenements were becoming less and less acceptable to the wealthier sections of the population. There was no space for creating residential squares on the London model but Mylne's Court (1684) and Mylne's Square (1690) off the Lawnmarket were attempts to provide more spacious housing conditions within restricted confines. The façades of these apartment blocks have more elegance and uniformity than their predecessors, reflecting the more demanding tastes and higher incomes of some of the city's inhabitants at this period. By the end of the seventeenth century it was evident to many people that Edinburgh needed more space for expansion, better housing and more impressive public buildings. Nevertheless, it was not until well into the eighteenth century that the processes of expansion and improvement were set in motion.

10

THE MAKING
OF EDINBURGH:
THE NEW TOWN

THE FIRST MOVES TOWARDS EXPANSION

WHEN the Jacobite army captured Edinburgh in 1745 the city was still largely confined within the Flodden wall although some suburban growth had taken place to the south. The city desperately needed room for expansion. It had no public buildings of note and was chronically short of space. Some tenements were in a dangerous condition. One collapsed in the early 1750s and others around it had to be demolished for safety. Ideas for improving the city were in the air after the failure of the '45 rebellion. A start was made in 1753 with the construction of the Royal Exchange, now the City Chambers, opposite St Giles. It replaced an older exchange built in 1683 to the east of Parliament House and destroyed by fire in 1700. It was designed as a meeting place for Edinburgh merchants and included a custom house, shops, coffee houses and printing works.

Residential squares had featured prominently in the expansion of London since the late-seventeenth century and had spread to English provincial towns. Early experiments along similar lines took place in a piecemeal fashion on the south side of Edinburgh. Argyle Square (c1742) and Brown's Square (1750s), both since demolished, were built in the area between the Greyfriars Church and the Old College of the University. These squares were small but a more impressive development was George Square, completed in the 1760s. Although the square is now dominated by the high-rise buildings of the University the eastern and western sides are largely unaltered, with their terraces of solid, no-nonsense Georgian houses. The scale on which George Square was constructed was a forerunner of the more ambitious schemes which were about to be developed north of the

192

Plate 52 The Royal Exchange, built in the mid-eighteenth century, was Edinburgh's first new public building in the scheme to improve the city

Old Town but expansion to the south of the city was hindered by lack of easy access to the High Street until the deep valley of the Cowgate was spanned by the construction of the South Bridge in 1788.

Because of the piecemeal nature of early suburban development south of the Cowgate there was little scope for large, integrated planning schemes. However, an ideal site for expansion existed on the gently-sloping ridge which ran parallel to the Old Town beyond the Nor Loch, provided that the land could be acquired and the deep valley separating it from the Old Town bridged. A leading figure behind the new plans was Provost George Drummond who published a set of proposals for extending the city in 1752. These formed the blueprint for the first New Town. In 1759 drainage of the Nor Loch was started and in 1763 work on the North Bridge was begun. In 1767 an Act of Parliament authorised an extension of the city's royalty to include the area known as Bearford's Parks on the far side of the Nor Loch, the road called the Lang Dykes (the future Princes Street) and other adjacent land which the city authorities had bought. All that was needed was a design for the New Town.

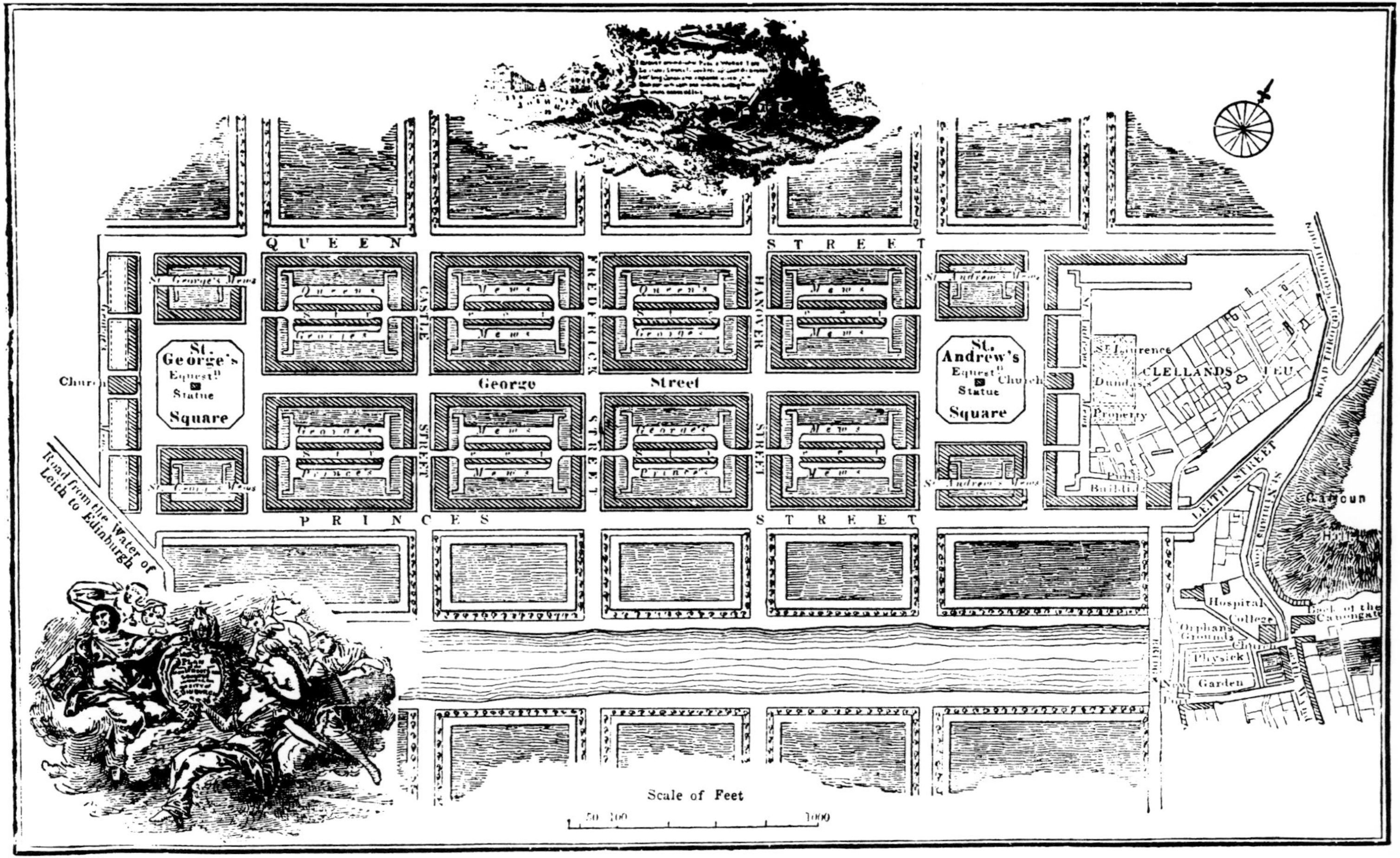

Fig 28 James Craig's original plan for Edinburgh's first New Town

CRAIG'S NEW TOWN

In 1766 a competition was held to select a plan. The winning entry was by James Craig, an unknown architect only 23 years old. His scheme was straightforward: a main street running east-west along the crest of the ridge linking a square at each end. On either side were two other streets running parallel to the central one while two narrower lanes ran between them. These minor streets gave access to mews and stables at the rear of the main properties and were designed to house the tradespeople who would provide services for the well-to-do inhabitants of the principal streets. Other thorough-fares intersected the five parallel streets at right angles to produce a grid plan.

Craig's plan has been criticised as dull, orthodox and unadventurous. Certainly he did not incorporate some of the new planning ideas which were currently in vogue, such as crescents and circuses. The success of his plan lies in its superb use of the site, with the ground falling away on either side of the central street giving fine views at each intersection of the Old Town on one hand and of the Firth of Forth on the other. The names of the streets in Craig's New Town symbolised the union of Scotland and England under the house of Hanover. The main avenue, George Street, named after the King, linked St Andrew and St George Squares. Parallel to George Street ran Queen Street and Princes Street. The narrower lanes between were named Rose and Thistle Street. Two of the cross streets were named after the House of Hanover and Frederick, George's son. Unfortunately for the symmetry of the design Edinburgh already had a George Square south of the Old Town (named after the architect's brother rather than the monarch!) To avoid confusion St George Square was renamed Charlotte Square after the Queen. The location of Craig's plan on the ground does not fit the site perfectly. It was impossible to locate St Andrew Square sufficiently far to the east to link it directly with the North Bridge as the city did not then own all the land west of Calton Hill. The line of the old road to Queensferry also impinged on the junction between Charlotte Square and Princes Street at the west end of the plan.

The construction of residential property began around St Andrew Square and gradually moved westwards. Two houses facing each other across a small courtyard near the east end of Thistle Street were the first to be built. They still survive, though dwarfed by later development. Their simple design and the open space between them give these houses an almost suburban air but this courtyard layout was not repeated in the side streets of Craig's town, probably

Plate 53 Hanover Street. The original bow-fronted design with central pediment survives above the modern shopfronts

Plate 54 The central block of the north side of Charlotte Square

because it took up too much space. The south and east sides of St Andrew Square retain much of their original character. The south side consists of a terrace of Georgian town houses which, while conforming generally in height and appearance, are all individual in materials, layout and design. Their rubble masonry has a distinctly vernacular air compared with the carefully-tooled ashlar of later houses in the New Town but they were designed to be covered with roughcast or stucco. The effect is attractive but was probably not what the developers originally had in mind. The city council made the mistake of applying only general guidelines relating to the height and width of the façades, and made no attempt to achieve uniformity of design. In fairness to them, at this stage of its development the New Town was very much a speculative venture and no builder was prepared to risk designing a complete row of houses with a uniform façade in case they should not be sold. Each house in the first phase of the development was built as an individual one-off venture.

Craig's plan included a church at the far sides of each square framing the vista down George Street. By a neat piece of manoeuvring Sir Laurence Dundas, who had amassed a fortune as Commissary General to the British army in Flanders during the 1750s, acquired the site for the church in St Andrew Square without the city council realising. He built himself a fine town house before anyone could protest! The result was a magnificent classical house set back from the square behind a courtyard and an attractive wrought-iron gateway. The council, accepting the house as a fait accompli, made the best of it by having the later buildings on either side designed as a matching pair, framing Dundas' house and giving it the appearance of a country mansion with a main block flanked by side pavilions. St Andrew's church was eventually built on the south side of George Street in a rather cramped location which fails to do justice to its fine classical façade.

As development proceeded westwards the city council succeeded in imposing more stringent building regulations while the success of the development encouraged builders to speculate more and construct unified groups of houses in advance of demand. As you walk westwards through Craig's town the façades become more uniform and the house fronts more stylish. In Hanover Street some plain bow-fronted houses survive above the modern shop-fronts but further west in North Castle Street this design has been embellished and perfected.

The masterpiece of the first New Town is Charlotte Square, a major achievement in European urban architecture. Charlotte Square is grand in conception but human in proportion. The city council commissioned Robert Adam, the foremost architect of his day, to design the square as a unified scheme. His plan, produced in 1791, was for palace façades with central classical pediments and projecting end blocks. The houses were to be further unified by ornamental features like balustrades, decorative panels and wrought iron railings. The square was built mainly between 1792 and the early-nineteenth century. The north side is closest to Adam's original design, though this is partly due to some careful twentieth-century restoration. During and after the original building alterations were made which departed from Adam's plan: doors and windows were changed and extra floors and dormer windows inserted in the roofs against his instructions. These variations do not, however, detract from the fine appearance of the square as a whole.

The square is dominated by St George's church – on its intended site unlike St Andrew's church – although the council tried to save money by dropping Adam's design in favour of a cheaper, plainer one by Robert Reid. A house on the north side of the square has been restored to its original condition by the National Trust for Scotland and its interior makes a fascinating contrast with that of Gladstone's Land in the Lawnmarket of the Old Town, emphasising the tremendous gap in style and material wealth which separated the first inhabitants of the New Town from the merchant burgesses of a century and a half before.

Much of the southern part of Craig's town has been heavily altered by later office and retail development although the street plan is unchanged. Modern shop fronts dominate Princes Street where only one or two of the original plain Georgian frontages remain above ground floor level. Many houses in George Street have been replaced by Victorian banks. The northern part of the New Town still preserves much of its original character though most of the buildings are occupied as offices rather than homes. Queen Street is relatively unchanged, many of its houses providing good examples of how, within the general building guidelines, it was still possible to achieve individuality of design in the detail of windows, doorways and decorative features. The western half of Thistle Street is lined with the tall, rather dour façades of houses for the less wealthy residents, though even these are impressive enough. As these buildings lack basement areas and front immediately on to the pavement they give the narrow street a rather austere appearance which presages later nineteenth-century tenement developments. In the mews behind them some of the coach houses at the rear of the main properties still survive, converted to garages.

In the Old Town there had been little social segregation;

everybody was too closely packed. The first New Town began a trend towards the creation of distinctive 'status areas' within the city which were inhabited by people from clearly-defined social strata and income levels. Although provision was made for tradesmen and small businesses in the side streets, Craig's New Town was designed as an upper-class residential suburb. The flowering of Edinburgh's cultural and intellectual life in the later-eighteenth and nineteenth centuries which was such a notable feature of the Scottish Enlightenment was increasingly centred on the New Town. As the middle classes moved out, the Old Town was abandoned to the poorer levels of society and many parts of it deteriorated into slums creating a problem which was not seriously tackled until post-1945 renovation and demolition. It proved impossible to keep retail businesses out of the New Town though. They started to encroach on the eastern end of Princes Street whose residents began looking further afield for new houses.

EARLY EXTENSIONS TO THE FIRST NEW TOWN

Craig's New Town was designed as a self-contained entity with no scope for further expansion, as is shown by the lack of access eastwards and westwards from the two squares. By the time that Charlotte Square was completed, however, it was clear that there was plenty of demand for further building. The area north and west of Craig's New Town was owned by four main proprietors. During the early-nineteenth century each of them developed their lands as new residential areas. These developments were separate but because they adjoin each other and the original New Town one can walk from one to the other without any sense of discontinuity. While Craig's town has an air of sequential development from east to west, as though the architects and builders had experimented as they went, by the time these later developments were planned they had decided exactly what they wanted and how to achieve it so that these districts have more homogeneity of design. They also incorporate ideas like crescents and circuses which were not used in the first new town.

Heriot's Hospital owned the biggest block of land north of Queen Street and in the 1820s they laid out a large extension to the New Town as a speculative venture. The plan was not dissimilar to Craig's: a central street (Great King Street) linked a square (Drummond Square) and a circus (Royal Circus) with other streets running parallel and at right angles to form a grid. Because the development is sited on sloping ground it is less easy to appreciate its overall unity than with Craig's town no matter how fine

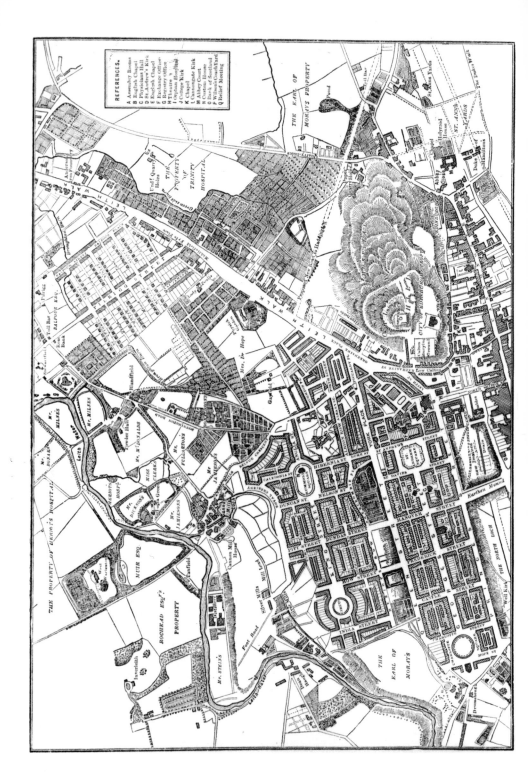

REFERENCES.

A Assembly Rooms
B English Chapel
C Physicians Hall
D St. Andrew's Kirk
E English Chapel
F Exchange offices
G Registry offices
H Theatre
I Orphan Hospital
J College Kirk
K Chapel
L Cannongate Kirk
M Abbey Court
N Custom House
O Bank of Scotland
P Wilson's Coach Yard
Q Relief Meeting

individual streets may appear. The principal streets with their long, uniform façades emphasised by extra height and decoration on the central and end blocks look very fine as they run along the slope but when the same idea is transferred to some of the steeply-sloping cross streets the effect does not work so well. The Heriot's development is more uniform architecturally than Craig's New Town not only because it was built over a shorter period but because stricter controls were imposed on the height and width of the frontage of each building; the kind of stone to be used was specified, and attic storeys and steeply-pitched roofs forbidden. There was still scope for individuality in the detail of doors, windows and decoration but only within a tightly-controlled framework. Buildings in some of the side streets are tenements rather than houses; the social distinctions follow Craig's pattern.

A block of land lying north and west of Charlotte Street was owned by the Earl of Moray, who began developing it for housing in 1822 when work on the Royal Circus was just starting. The Moray estate was to be a high-class residential development and the well-known architect James Gillespie Graham was commissioned to design the façades in great detail, down to the railings, to ensure absolute uniformity. The site was an awkward wedge-shaped one and instead of a grid layout the novel plan of a crescent, a double crescent and an eight-sided circus linked by short connecting streets was adopted. Because the earl specified the design so closely, Moray Place, the circus, is the most impressive private housing development in the city. Charlotte Square has a simpler classical style but Moray Place is more imposing, perhaps a little too heavy in appearance to be quite comfortable for private residences but a magnificent achievement nonetheless. Moray Place fails to achieve the same impact as Charlotte Square today because the mature trees in the central gardens prevent you from seeing the whole design.

THE CITY EXPANDS: EDINBURGH'S INNER SUBURBS

The early New Town was surrounded by many small estates whose proprietors, during the first half of the nineteenth century, became increasingly interested in selling their properties for housing. Beyond the west end of Princes Street the Coates estate was developed from the 1820s. Beyond the Moray estate further growth to the north-

Fig 29 A plan of the New Town in 1804. The Heriot's Hospital development is well advanced, but the Earl of Moray's property has not yet been built on

west was blocked by the ravine of the Water of Leith. Sir Henry Raeburn, the famous portrait painter, began to develop land on the far side from 1814. Ann Street, named after his wife, has terraced town houses of different sizes with a picturesque rural aspect, unusual for Edinburgh's New Town, created by laying out large front gardens whose greenery blends in well with the wooded valley side below. This area remained difficult of access until Sir John Learmonth, provost of Edinburgh, financed the building of the Dean Bridge, designed by Thomas Telford, which was finished in 1834.

In the mid-nineteenth century, when the New Town was being extended northwards and westwards, Edinburgh was also growing to the south. The most rapid phase of expansion occurred from the 1860s and 1870s. Much of the development, in areas like Grange and Morningside, took the form of substantial detached and semi-detached villas set in their own large gardens, a style of housing which was becoming more fashionable than terraced town houses. An example of the exclusive nature of some of these villa developments is Blacket Place in Newington. Here a group of villas, designed by James Gillespie Graham, was laid out between 1825 and 1860 in a leafy rustic setting. The entrances were provided with lodges whose gates were shut at night to ensure privacy. Residents could enjoy the peacefulness of a country dwelling combined with ready access to the city.

At the same period the first of Edinburgh's tenement areas was being laid out. Sir George Warrender's estate of Bruntsfield had been leapfrogged by expanding villa development in Grange to the south. Although only a short walk from George Square across the open parkland of the Meadows the area was still rural in the 1860s. The original plan was to build a mixture of terraced houses and large detached villas. Only a handful of terraced houses were actually built and the plan was changed to the construction of high-status tenements for middle-class occupiers. The building of the residential districts which came to be known as Bruntsfield, Marchmont and Warrender was fairly continuous during the last quarter of the nineteenth century and the early years of the twentieth. The earlier tenements, as in Marchmont Crescent, are richly ornamented in a Scots baronial style with turrets, crow-stepped gables and tall chimneys. The corner blocks are emphasised by towers with conical roofs while the use of bow fronts breaks up the main façades and are particularly effective when seen in long, sweeping curves as in Warrender Park Road. Later tenements, from early in the present century, were plainer and more sombre.

In the later-nineteenth century Edinburgh also began to acquire distinctive working-class districts in two main areas. One formed a wedge running south-west from the city centre, extending outwards from Fountainbridge on either side of Dalry Road. The other lay between Edinburgh and Leith extending out towards Abbeyhill. In addition smaller enclaves of working-class housing were built throughout the city. A distinctive type of housing in some of these areas were the model dwellings created by the Edinburgh Co-operative Building Company and other housing associations. The aim of these was to provide a good standard of housing for better-off artisan families. The prototype for these developments was Rosebank Cottages in Fountainbridge, originally built to house railway workers and now functioning as local authority accommodation. The houses were terraced flats on two levels. From a distance they appear to be two-storey houses but closer inspection shows that they are divided into upper and lower flats entered from separate streets. A larger area of these flats was the Colonies in Stockbridge but similar flatted housing was built in Abbeyhill, Leith and elsewhere. More widespread in the working-class areas were four-storey tenement blocks plainer and with smaller flats than the higher-status ones of Bruntsfield and Warrender. Many of them, in areas like St Leonards on the fringe of the Old Town, were demolished in the 1960s but more recently the trend has been to refurbish them with the aid of local authority grants.

Despite these developments, Edinburgh's inner suburbs still contained a good deal of open space. A feature of these areas is the number of private schools in their own extensive grounds. The model which influenced many of them was George Heriot's Hospital between the Castle and George Square. 'Jingling Geordie' Heriot was a wealthy Edinburgh goldsmith. When he died he left funds for the construction of a school for orphans. The resulting building, designed by the master mason William Wallace and constructed between 1628 and the Restoration, is Scotland's finest early Renaissance building. It is laid out around a courtyard and framed by battlemented corner towers. In the nineteenth century a number of other schools were built among Edinburgh's inner suburbs. Beyond Haymarket is Donaldson's school for the deaf. Built in the 1840s and early 1850s, its design owes a good deal to Heriot's though the Tudor and Jacobean decoration is more exuberant. Daniel Stewart's College on Queensferry Road, which dates from the same period, also harks back to the style of Heriot's. Other schools used classical styles, such as the Royal High School on Calton Hill and the rather austere Edinburgh Academy on the northern edge of the New Town. Grandest of all is Fettes College, north of the Dean

Bridge, which is framed by a long avenue of trees, and incorporates details reminiscent of a French château.

THE OUTER SUBURBS: VILLAGE EDINBURGH

The expansion of Edinburgh in the late-nineteenth and early-twentieth century, especially to the south and west, was facilitated by the development of horse-drawn omnibuses and a suburban railway network. In 1884 the Edinburgh Suburban & Southside Junction Railway was opened, encouraging suburban expansion in a broad arc to the south of the city from Duddingston to Morningside. In 1901 a branch line was built to connect the village of Corstorphine, west of Edinburgh, with the city centre. Another line, following the Water of Leith through Colinton, Currie, Juniper Green and Balerno turned a string of small industrial villages into a broad ribbon of suburban development. To the north the railway created the villa colonies of Barnton and Davidson's Mains at the end of the nineteenth century.

The area around eighteenth-century Edinburgh, over which the suburbs spread in the nineteenth and twentieth centuries, had some distinctive features which were incorporated in the expanding city. The landownership pattern was fragmented with many small estates each with its tower house or mansion. In the early-seventeenth century a French visitor to Edinburgh estimated that there were at least a hundred country seats within a radius of two leagues of the city. Some of these houses have survived within their own areas of parkland. Prestonfield House, a seventeenth-century mansion now used as a hotel, has one of the finest settings, overlooked by the crags of Arthur's Seat. Others, like the fifteenth-century tower at Liberton, which stands within a later farmstead, have fared less well. Many towers were later extended into more substantial mansions, like Lauriston Castle and Craigcrook Castle, both within the north-western suburbs.

A second feature of the outlying districts was the extensive areas of open country on the volcanic hills. Too steep to build on, many still survive as public parks, wedges of wild countryside which break up the suburban residential districts. Arthur's Seat and the Queen's Park, in ancient times an area of sanctuary belonging to Holyrood Abbey, was acquired by the Crown in 1846 and preserved from development. It must be the most topographically exciting urban park in Britain. Although rising to only just over 250m (820ft), Arthur's Seat and its surrounding crags have more character than many Highland mountains thanks to the complex geology of this extinct volcano. Further away from the city centre were Blackford Hill, the Braid Hills, Corstorphine Hill, and the Craiglockhart Hills. Most impressive of all was Hillend Park, including the imposing summits of the northern end of the Pentlands, which was gifted to the city as a recreation area.

As well as mansions, towers and parklands Edinburgh was also surrounded by villages and hamlets, each a distinctive community. Some have vanished entirely, their very names having been forgotten like the settlements of Newcampbeltown and Westerhall which were obliterated by the close-packed tenements of Marchmont. Others retained their identity despite being engulfed by the suburbs. Duddingston, on the south-eastern side of Arthur's Seat, is a good example. In the eighteenth century it was a settlement of weavers, coal carriers and labourers. Although little more than 3km (2 miles) from the centre of the city Duddingston still preserves its village atmosphere. The community focusses on the Norman parish church on a rocky knoll overlooking a small reed-fringed loch. Beyond the church is the main street of the village. At one end is the Sheep Heid Inn, one of Scotland's oldest hostelries, patronised by monarchs in the past, while at the other is the house in which Prince Charles Edward Stuart, the Young Pretender, stayed before the Battle of Prestonpans in 1745.

West of the city centre Corstorphine was another rural community focussing on the old castle of the Forrester family and the collegiate church which they endowed. The castle has vanished but its dovecot, a seventeenth-century dower house built by the family, and the picturesque old church still survive. In the eighteenth century Corstorphine enjoyed a period of popularity as a spa centre with a special stagecoach service several times a day from Edinburgh. Unfortunately, the deepening of a nearby stream channel caused the mineral well that had supplied the spa water to dry up. By the end of the nineteenth century a regular horse bus service and later the railway linked Corstorphine more closely with the nearby city and the area around the village was developed with villas and tenements.

Other villages were more industrial in character. Dean Village, hidden in the gorge of the Water of Leith, on the northern fringes of the first New Town, is often missed by visitors. The best view of it is from the parapet of Telford's Dean Bridge. The nearest source of water power to the city, this was a milling centre from at least the twelfth century. At one time there were eleven water-powered grain mills and two granaries here. The influence of the incorporation of baxters or bakers is still evident. Bell's Brae House, built as an inn in 1640, was used as their meeting place. Close by is the baxters' tolbooth, their official headquarters, also built in the seventeenth century. Careful restoration of many of the older buildings and the sensitive construction of new ones which blend in well with them has helped to preserve the distinctive character of the community. The construction of the Dean Bridge re-routed the main road to Queensferry and by-passed the settlement but prior to this all traffic going in this direction dropped down Bell's Brae into the gorge, crossed the Water of Leith on a narrow, single-arched bridge and climbed up the other side.

There were communities along the coast too. Cramond, at the mouth of the River Almond, was a significant port in the nineteenth century. Iron forges a short way up the river provided employment and many of the workers lived in the whitewashed cottages along the quay which, restored in the 1960s, form an attractive focus to the settlement today. Newhaven started as a naval dockyard in the sixteenth century but developed into a fishing harbour. The Newhaven fishwives, with their distinctive striped costumes, were a common sight in the centre of Edinburgh where they sold the fish that their menfolk had caught. Further east, Portobello was an area of open heath, the Figgate Whins, in the early-eighteenth century. Around 1742 a retired sailor built himself a cottage here naming it after the Spanish town sacked by the British in 1739. In 1763 an Edinburgh builder leased some adjacent ground and started a brickworks using local clay. This was followed by two pottery factories and the north-west end of Portobello became a thriving industrial centre. From the late-eighteenth century, however, Porto-bello also developed as a fashionable sea-bathing resort. The elegant Georgian summer houses of wealthy Edinburgh residents and the more opulent Victorian villas that succeeded them help to give Portobello its distinctive character. In later times, when improved communications made more distant resorts fashionable, Portobello went down-market catering for day trippers from Edinburgh's working classes. The careful modern renovation of some of its best buildings is helping to rehabilitate it today.

HERITAGE, PLANNING AND CONSERVATION

Despite its architectural wealth, Edinburgh has not escaped un-scathed from post-war property development. Many old buildings badly needed demolition and many of the new ones which have replaced them have been of great architectural merit. The desirability of some changes has, however, been questionable. For instance, it was not surprising that the civic authorities should have sanctioned

Plate 55 White Horse Close, Canongate. An example of sensitive post-war restoration of old property

the demolition of St James Square in the 1960s. It was one of the earliest squares in the New Town, squeezed between Register House, the head of Leith Walk and the eastern side of St Andrew Square. However, it had deteriorated badly and the area had gone down-market socially while its austere architecture made it less attractive than other parts of the New Town. Even so, its replacement by the St James' Centre, an enclosed shopping and hotel complex, was particularly insensitive. Not only does it present a blank, warehouse-like exterior when seen close to but it ruins the vista across the South Bridge which was formerly framed by Register House, and also intrudes gracelessly upon the skyline of the city when seen from the north.

One of the worst examples of 1960s planning took place on the south side of the city centre, the culprits being the expanding University and a scheme for an inner ring road which, in the event, was never built. The removal of the mid-eighteenth-century town houses on the south side of George Square to make way for the new University library and arts and social science faculty buildings, and the way in which the David Hume and Appleton Tower blocks dominated the skyline, aroused a good deal of protest. As the University expanded what had once been a working-class area with a strong sense of community was largely destroyed. The demolition of extensive areas of early tenement properties with attractive rear tower staircases in Bristo Street and Potterrow was accomplished with no better result than to turn the open space so created into a huge car park.

Even the Royal Mile did not escape the hand of the developer. Admittedly, a lot of work was needing to be done in the centre of the Old Town. By the 1950s many tenements had deteriorated into slums and successful efforts were made to renovate many of them. The block above Deacon Brodie's Tavern, at the corner of Lawnmarket and Bank Street, is a good example. Many slums in the Canongate were also restored while several new buildings incorporated the old arcading which had been a feature of the earlier tenements. The reconstruction of White Horse Close at the foot of the Canongate in the 1950s was particularly attractive. Higher up at Chessel's Court the mid-eighteenth century buildings were restored in the 1960s and the courtyard was finished off by the insertion of new blocks of flats in a style in keeping with the old. By contrast, the new block on the corner of Lawnmarket and George IV Bridge which houses the Lothian Regional Council's offices clashes painfully with the earlier buildings around it. The village communities of suburban Edinburgh, vociferously middle-class, have been more successful at resisting the less desirable aspects of change. Vigorous activity by local heritage trusts and amenity societies has led to the cores of many old communities, such as Cramond and Duddingston, being designated as conservation areas.

The excesses of this period have given way to a more sensitive approach which has placed a greater emphasis on renovation and restoration along with the construction of buildings which are in sympathy with the surrounding townscape. A good example can be seen in Nicholson Street on the south side of the city centre on the fringe of the area which has been altered so drastically by the expansion of the University. Here, some of the existing terraced houses and tenements have been renovated and new buildings in a neo eighteenth-century style inserted in the spaces between them. There will be major conservation problems in the future though. The buildings in Craig's New Town are starting to show their age and substantial investment of capital and effort will be needed to maintain them to an acceptable standard.

CONCLUSION:
THE MODERN
LANDSCAPE, HERITAGE
AND THE FUTURE

T HE impact of modern technology means that landscape
change in Britain during the present century has proceeded at a
much faster rate than ever before. The Lothians and the Borders have
been affected less drastically than many parts of the country. Even
so, many changes have occurred. Some have already been considered; the decline or disappearance of industries like coal mining
and oil shale extraction that flourished in the nineteenth and early-
twentieth centuries, or the run down of the railway network in the
post-war period. The landscaping of some of the most blighted
industrial sites has been a positive contribution to visual amenity.
Many of the railways which were fresh scars on the landscape only
a century ago are now, disused and grassed over, blending gently
into their surroundings. The continued suburban growth of Edinburgh has encroached on the countryside while increased commuting
to the city by car has led to the expansion of housing developments
in burghs like Haddington, Linlithgow and Peebles. The increased
need for energy has produced huge power stations which dominate
the landscape for miles around like the coal-fired one at Cockenzie
and the nuclear-powered one at Torness near Dunbar.

Many recent changes in the landscape have been attractive or at
least have had their beneficial side. Growing demand for water for
Edinburgh and other Lothian towns has, from the later-nineteenth
century, led to the building of a series of reservoirs among the nearby
hills. At first the valleys of the Pentland Hills, a short distance beyond
the city's southern suburbs, were utilised. Here the alterations in the
landscape have been positive. Whether viewed from the surrounding
hilltops or from the valley floor few would argue that developments

like Glencorse Reservoir, with its fringe of pine trees, do not add interest and variety to the scene. Later schemes tapped the northern fringes of the Moorfoots but then, as demand increased, supplies were sought further afield. Early in the present century a dam was completed in the Talla valley among the Tweedsmuir Hills and a new reservoir, much larger than any in the Pentlands, was constructed in this deep glacially-scoured valley. In the 1960s a second reservoir on a similar scale was added in the neighbouring Fruid valley. There was considerable concern over the loss of salmon spawning grounds and their effects on the flow of the River Tweed, but developments like these will, in time, become part of the landscape.

The Forestry Commission have developed parts of the Borders for large-scale conifer plantations. In many cases the results have been attractive, as at Glentress Forest, north of Peebles, where the plantations have been established over ground of varied topography and contain a mixture of tree species. Glentress and most other Border forests are substantial blocks of planting but they do not dominate the landscape. Wauchope Forest, at the head of the Jed Water on the northern slopes of the Cheviots, is on an altogether greater scale. An extension of the immense forest of Kielder in Northumberland, you can walk through it for a dozen kilometres and see little but newly-planted conifers. Afforestation on this scale

Plate 56 Large-scale planting of conifers by the Forestry Commission has transformed the open landscape of many parts of the Border hills in recent years

Plate 57 The rolling hill country of the Borders near Melrose

is bound to obliterate much of the previous landscape, as has happened with the prehistoric field system at Tamshiel Rig (644060).

Landscapes have always changed and must continue to evolve; if they are fossilised they become mere artificial museum pieces. Yet this evolution must be controlled if the best of the landscape heritage from earlier centuries is to be preserved. To achieve this we need to know how and why the landscapes of the past, and their remnants which survive today, have been created. In a single short book it has only been possible to outline the main processes involved in creating the present landscape heritage of Edinburgh and the Borders. Yet even at this level the limitations of present knowledge will have become evident to the reader.

There is tremendous scope for further research into how the historic landscapes of this region, and indeed other parts of Scotland, have evolved. Excavation, even on a small scale, requires considerable finance and manpower. However, patient work in archives and libraries, if time consuming, is at least cheap. Best of all, studying the landscape itself through fieldwork combines intellectual and physical exercise. Even an individual working alone, with a keen eye and a questioning mind, can make important contributions to our understanding and appreciation of how the landscape has developed.

BIBLIOGRAPHY

T HIS guide to further reading mainly covers books which are still in print or have been published fairly recently and should be widely available from libraries.

For general reading on many aspects of the landscape of Edinburgh and the Borders the various volumes of the Royal Commission on the Ancient and Historical Monuments of Scotland provide a wealth of information, particularly the later ones. The series comprises Berwickshire (1915), East Lothian (1924), Mid and West Lothian (1929), the City of Edinburgh (1951), Roxburghshire (2 vols 1956), Selkirk (1957), and Peebles-shire (2 vols 1967).

A good general introduction is Baldwin, J. R., *Exploring Scotland's Heritage: Lothian and the Borders* (HMSO, 1985)

Chapter 1
Craig, G. Y. & Duff, P. M., *The geology of the Lothians and South East Scotland* (Edinburgh, 1975)
Greig, D. C., *British Regional Geology* 'The south of Scotland' (HMSO, 1971)
MacGregor, M. & A. G., *British Regional Geology* 'The Midland Valley of Scotland' (HMSO, 1948)
Sissons, J. B., *Scotland* (London, 1976)
Whittow, J. B., *Geology and scenery in Scotland* (London, 1977)

Chapter 2
Feachem, R. W., *The North Britons* (London, 1965)
Keppie, L., *Scotland's Roman remains* (Edinburgh, 1988)
Ritchie, G. & R., *Scotland: archaeology and early history* (London, 1985)

Chapter 3
Dodgshon, R. A., *Land and society in early Scotland* (Oxford, 1981)
Parry, M. L. & Slater, T. R. (eds), *The making of the Scottish countryside* (London, 1980)
Whyte, I. D., *Agriculture and society in seventeenth-century Scotland* (Edinburgh, 1979)

Chapter 4
MacGibbon D. & Ross, T., *The ecclesiastical architecture of Scotland*. 3 vols (Edinburgh, 1887–92)

MacWilliam, C. & Eilson, C., *Lothian* (London, 1978)

Thomas C., *The early Christian archaeology of North Britain* (London, 1971)

Chapter 5

Cruden, S., *The Scottish castle* (London, 1973)

Dunbar, J. G., *The historic architecture of Scotland* (London, 1978)

MacGibbon, D. & Ross, T., *The castellated and domestic architecture of Scotland*. 5 vols (Edinburgh 1887–92)

MacWilliam, C. & Wilson, C., *Lothian* (London, 1978)

Tranter, N., *The fortified house in Scotland*. Vol. 1. (London, 1962)

Chapter 6

Handley, J. E., *Scottish farming in the eighteenth century* (Edinburgh, 1953)

Handley, J. E., *The Agricultural Revolution in Scotland* (Edinburgh, 1963)

Whyte, I. D., *Agriculture and society in seventeenth-century Scotland* (Edinburgh, 1979)

Chapter 7

Thomas, J., *The North British Railway*. 2 vols (Newton Abbot, 1968 & 1975)

Thomas, J., *A regional history of the railways of Great Britain*. Vol. 6. (Newton Abbot, 1971)

Chapter 8

Adams, I. H., *The making of urban Scotland* (London, 1978)

Gulvin, C., *The Tweedmakers* (Newton Abbot, 1973)

Hume, J., *The industrial archaeology of Scotland: the Lowlands and the Borders* (London, 1978)

Shaw, J., *Water power in Scotland* (Edinburgh, 1984)

Skinner, B. C., *The lime industry in the Lothians* (Edinburgh, 1969)

Chapter 9

Daiches, D., *Edinburgh* (London, 1978)

Gifford, J. McWilliam, C, Walker, D., *Edinburgh* (London, 1985)

McKean, C., *Edinburgh: an illustrated architectural guide* (Edinburgh, 1982)

Chapter 10

Cant, M., *Villages of Edinburgh*. 2 vols (Edinburgh, 1986 & 1987)

McKean, C., *Edinburgh: an illustrated architectural guide* (Edinburgh, 1982)

Youngson, A. J., *The making of classical Edinburgh* (Edinburgh, 1966)

INDEX